GOING FORTH

OMER DEGRIJSE, C.I.C.M.

GOING FORTH

Missionary Consciousness in Third World Catholic Churches

Maryknoll, New York 10545

The Catholic Foreign Mission Society of America (Maryknoll) recruits and trains people for overseas missionary service. Through Orbis Books Maryknoll aims to foster the international dialogue that is essential to mission. The books published, however, reflect the opinions of their authors and are not meant to represent the official position of the society.

Copyright © 1984 Orbis Books, Maryknoll, NY 10545
All rights reserved
Manufactured in the United States of America

Manuscript Editor: William E. Jerman

Library of Congress Cataloging in Publication Data

Degrijse, Omer, 1913-
   Going forth: missionary consciousness in Third World Catholic Churches.

   1. Catholic Church—Missions—History—20th century.
2. Catholic Church—Developing countries.   I. Title.
BV2185.D43   1984   266'.023'1724   83-19337
ISBN 0-88344-427-5 (pbk.)

Going forth, therefore,
make disciples of all nations,
baptizing them in the name of the Father
and of the Son and of the Holy Spirit,
teaching them to observe
all that I have commanded you;
and lo, I am with you always,
to the close of the age.
[Matt. 28: 19-20]

CONTENTS

FOREWORD ix
ABBREVIATIONS AND ACRONYMS xi

CHAPTER ONE
TOWARD A NEW UNDERSTANDING OF MISSION 1

Why the Young Churches Have to Become Missionary 3
Impact of the 1974 Synod of Bishops 6
The Rise of the Third Church 11
Church Statistics 14
Expansion of the Religious Life in Africa, Asia, and
    Oceania 17
Institutional Commitment to Mission 19

CHAPTER TWO
THE RISE OF MISSIONARY CONSCIOUSNESS
IN AFRICA 23

General Survey 23
African Religious in the Service of Mission 28

CHAPTER THREE
THE RISE OF MISSIONARY CONSCIOUSNESS
IN ASIA 34

General Survey 34
The Philippines 37
India 42
Korea 49

Japan 51
Vietnam 53
Sri Lanka 55

CHAPTER FOUR
THE RISE OF MISSIONARY CONSCIOUSNESS IN LATIN AMERICA 57

Missionary Commitment *ad extra* 58
Mexico 61
Colombia 62
Brazil 63
Other Latin American Countries 65
The Role of Puebla 66
The Lima Document 67

CHAPTER FIVE
FINAL CONSIDERATIONS 71

Findings 71
Conclusion 91

INDEX 93

FOREWORD

The communications media enable us to follow major events on a worldwide scope. But in more subtle matters evolution has been so fast that at times we get to know only today what has been going on for years in other continents.

This is true of the life of the universal church, especially with regard to the part of the church that we have recently begun to call the "third church"—namely, the churches of Africa, Asia, Latin America, and Oceania, distinguishing them from the long-established Eastern and Western churches.[1]

The rise of the missionary consciousness of the third church is a recent phenomenon, still unknown to many. A look at the missionary impulse in Third World churches will provoke not a few surprises.

The data used in this study have been gathered from many sources. Some figures are only approximate. Sources are not always reliable. In fact this survey often refers to what was verifiable two or three years earlier. At times statistics are available only some years after the facts. This is the case, for example, with the *Annuarium Statisticum Ecclesiae.* Consequently, the missionary commitment of Third World churches is further advanced than is portrayed in this study.

A few years ago, Walbert Bühlmann's book *The Coming of the Third Church* surprised many.[2] In it he fills in a picture of the non-Western churches and shows that the center of gravity within the universal church is moving from North to South and East. The third church is becoming the most dynamic wing of the universal church. It is a church of hope. It proves it most clearly by becoming a missionary church.

The missionary involvement of Third World churches challenges the older Christian churches, which have been suffering from a sort of missionary fatigue. The Third World churches can help the Western churches to recover their self-confidence and their missionary dynamism. The Third World churches are the fruit of the missionary dedication of Western missionaries. Today they express their readiness to evangelize the Western churches, if only by reminding them that the proclamation of the good news is a mission entrusted to all the churches. It remains mandatory for the Western churches as well.[3]

Notes

1. The term "Third World church" or "third church" refers to the Christian churches of Africa, Asia, Latin America, and Oceania. It is not, however, perfectly coincident with the Third World: Japan, for example, belongs to the third church, but not to the Third World. The term "young churches" applies especially to the churches in Africa, Asia, and Oceania.

2. *The Coming of the Third Church: An Analysis of the Present and Future of the Church* (Maryknoll, N.Y.: Orbis, 1974).

3. The present study is restricted to a survey of Catholic mission. The missionary movement is equally strong in the Protestant (especially Evangelical) and Anglican young churches.

ABBREVIATIONS AND ACRONYMS

A.G.   *Ad Gentes* (Vatican II)

AMECEA Association of Member Episcopal Conferences of Eastern Africa

C.D.   *Christus Dominus* (Vatican II)

CELAM   *Consejo Episcopal Latinoamericano,* Latin American Episcopal Conference

CLAR   *Conferencia Latinoamericana de Religiosos,* Latin American Conference of Religious

COMLA   *Congreso Misionero Latinoamericano,* Latin American Mission Congress

E.N.   *Evangelii Nuntiandi* (Apostolic Exhortation on Evangelization in the Modern World, December 8, 1975)

FABC   Federation of Asian Bishops' Conferences

G.S.   *Gaudium et Spes* (Vatican II)

L.G.   *Lumen Gentium* (Vatican II)

P.C.   *Perfectae Caritatis* (Vatican II)

SECAM   Symposium of Episcopal Conferences of Africa and Madagascar

GOING FORTH

CHAPTER ONE

TOWARD A NEW UNDERSTANDING OF MISSION

Until very recently, mission was the undertaking of the well-established Western churches. How could it have been otherwise? To a world that did not know Christ, the gospel could be proclaimed only by missionaries sent out by churches that had professed the faith for centuries. Missionaries from Europe, and later from North America, brought the good news to other parts of the world.

The main concern of evangelizers was conversion to Christ, the salvation of souls, the forming of Christian communities. It took a long time for missionaries to understand that their first goal should be the establishing of local churches, which in their turn should become responsible for continued evangelization. Little or no attention was paid to this from the sixteenth to the eighteenth centuries under the Spanish and Portuguese Patronato (Padroado) system. With the foundation of the Propaganda Fide in 1622, the popes tried to get a firmer hold on mission work and have it follow a new course. A famous Instruction (1659) was entrusted to Bishop Pierre Lambert de la Motte, Bishop François Pallu, and their fellow workers of the Foreign Missions of Paris, the principal agents for carrying out the new policy. It stated that they should give priority to the formation of a local clergy, with a view to founding local churches. It also stipulated that the cultural and religious traditions of an evangelized people should be taken into account. This signaled a radical revolution in missionary methods. The Vatican carried on a long-lasting struggle with the Spanish and Portuguese governments over the control of missions and the application of the new methods.

Only during the nineteenth century, when the Spanish and Portuguese dominion had waned, did the popes fully succeed in getting a firm hold on missionary policy. In his Instruction *Neminem Profecto* (1845) Gregory XVI, the great missionary pope of that century, stated that in their work of evangelization missionaries had to give priority to the formation of a local clergy.

The second half of the nineteenth century witnessed a missionary expansion unprecedented in church history. Missionaries set out for all parts of the world, including newly discovered regions. However, their main purpose was still the conversion of "pagans," the administration of sacraments, the building of Christian communities. Less attention was paid to the training of a local clergy. The founding of local churches was still very far away.

The vigorous action and the hard language of Benedict XV in his encyclical *Maximum Illud* (1919) and of Pius XI in his encyclical *Rerum Ecclesiae* (1926), both inspired by the clear-sighted and energetic Cardinal van Rossum, were needed to bring about a change in this situation. Absolute priority was now given to the building of seminaries for indigenous priests. Pius XI started to speed up the appointment of native bishops and the establishment of local churches. At the Second Vatican council, 150 Asian and African bishops were present.

Vatican II showed how difficult it was to shift from the traditional view on mission to a new one. Only during the last session did the conciliar fathers realize that mission should no longer be seen as an enterprise of the Western churches, and that the young churches ought to occupy a central place in the decree on the missionary activity of the church (*Ad Gentes*). From being the object of mission the young churches became its subject. Thus one chapter (chap. 3), on the young churches, was added to *Ad Gentes*. This indicates an important change of perspective. The mission of missionaries becomes the mission of the young churches. But the other chapters do not sufficiently take account of this point. In them mission is still predominantly considered to be the task of Western missionary institutes. Chapter 6 describes missionary cooperation very much as a one-way activity.

Why the Young Churches Have to Become Missionary

The renewed understanding of mission was a logical consequence of the Vatican II ecclesiology, especially of the conciliar doctrine on the particular churches, one of its main "discoveries." The people of God is described as a messianic people (L.G. n. 9). Several passages state that the entire church is missionary and that evangelization is a fundamental duty of the people of God (L.G. n. 17; A.G. n. 35, 36). It is the duty of all the members of the church: the pope, the bishops (A.G. n. 38), the priests (A.G. n. 39), the religious (A.G. n. 40), the laity (A.G. n. 41). Every Christian community must develop a missionary dimension:

> The grace of renewal cannot flourish in communities unless each of them extends the range of its charity to the ends of the earth, and devotes to those far off a concern similar to that which it bestows on those who are its own members [A.G. n. 37].

An important passage in *Lumen Gentium* states that the particular churches are "fashioned after the model of the universal church. In and from such individual churches there comes into being the one and only Catholic Church" (n. 23). They are the localized universal church. Hence, like the universal church, they have to be entirely missionary. Mission pertains to the very being of the local church. The teaching is spelled out in *Ad Gentes*:

> In order that this missionary zeal may flourish among their native members, it is very fitting that the young churches should really participate, as soon as possible, in the universal

missionary work of the church. Let them send their own missionaries to proclaim the gospel all over the world, even though they themselves are suffering from a shortage of clergy. For their communion with the universal church reaches a certain measure of completion where they themselves take an active part in missionary activity toward other nations [n. 20].

The young churches must live in communion with the universal church:

> Let the young churches preserve an intimate communion with the church universal. They should embed [its] traditions in their own culture, thereby increasing the life of the mystical body by a certain mutual exchange of energies. Hence, stress should be laid on those theological, psychological, and human elements which can contribute to fostering this sense of communion with the universal church [A.G. n. 19].

The young churches should progressively evolve toward self-reliance and the capability to assist others:

> The whole young church should render one vital and firm witness to Christ, and thus become a shining beacon of the salvation which has come to us in Christ [A.G. n. 21].

The council stated repeatedly that the church must incarnate itself in non-Western cultures; no longer may it be a stranger to "the nations." Thus diversity within the universal church is being accepted. New insights and experiences will grow as a result of the incarnation of the good news in diverse cultures. The young churches have the most important role to play in this matter. Their own spiritual values can enrich the universal church.

> The individual young churches, adorned with their own traditions, will have their own place in the ecclesial communion, without prejudice to the primacy of St. Peter's See, which presides over the entire assembly of charity [A.G. n. 22].

The ecclesiology of Vatican II has lifted the young churches from their marginality, their "second-class" ranking. They become autonomous, equal, responsible, particular churches within the universal church, which is the worldwide communion of particular churches.

The teaching on the particular churches led to a renewed insight into the collegial character of the church. Not the pope only, but the whole college of bishops, under the leadership of the pope, is responsible for the mission of the church in the world. Various texts of the council confer the responsibility for the evangelization of the world on the entire college of bishops, every episcopal conference, and every bishop; hence also every church:

> As members of the body of bishops which succeeded to the college of Apostles, all bishops are consecrated not just for some one diocese, but for the salvation of the entire world. Christ's mandate to preach the gospel to every creature (Mark 16:15) primarily and immediately concerns them, with Peter and under Peter. From this fact arises that communion and cooperation between churches which is so necessary today for carrying on the work of evangelization. In virtue of this communion, individual churches carry a responsibility for all the others. They make their necessities known to one another, and keep one another mutually informed regarding their affairs [A.G. n. 38; see L.G. n. 23].

St. Paul's teaching on the Body of Christ confirms that the churches care for each other, and the council states:

> Between all the parts of the church there remains a bond of close communion with respect to spiritual riches, apostolic works, and temporal resources [L.G. n. 13; C.D. n. 6].

All churches are summoned to generosity and mutual exchange. Each one of them has something to give and something to receive. No church can retire within itself. Universal openness belongs to its essence. The building of the church in Kinshasa is not only the responsibility of the local bishop and his community; it is also the concern of the universal church and of the other local churches. For its own part, the Christian community of Kinshasa cannot remain indifferent to the needs of the churches in Europe and Asia.

The conciliar ecclesiology could not but invite the young churches to reflect on these insights, to open up new perspectives, and to stimulate their missionary consciousness.

Impact of the 1974 Synod of Bishops

At the close of Vatican II, who was aware of the potential, the dynamics—if not to say dynamite—hidden in the conciliar doctrine? Who foresaw the church's inner evolution in the years to come?

Even if the fundamental aspects of the missiology of Vatican II remained always valid, scarcely ten years later some aspects of the *Ad Gentes* missionary vision appeared outdated already. Mission, in 1965 still considered a task of the Western churches, is fully becoming an undertaking of the young churches. Western missionaries and missionary institutes have faded into the background. As the Third World emancipated itself from the Western world during this period, so also the "mission church" freed itself from the Western church. As the map of the world and world history were thoroughly modified by the rise of the Third World, so also there occurred a radical change in the image of the universal church.

In 1973 there were 170 African and 144 Asian bishops. Some five years later, 271 of the 432 bishops of Africa were Africans, and 331 of the 467 bishops of Asia were Asian. An authentic African, Asian, and Latin American church started to develop as a result of the Vatican II teaching on the appropriateness of diversity within the church.

An event of vast importance for the evolution of the postconciliar church was the 1974 synod of bishops, which dealt with "Evangelization in the Contemporary World." This synod was very well prepared for, all over the world, but especially in Third World churches. Every local church, every bishops' conference had been requested to study the problem of evangelization, proceeding from an analysis of the local situation. Then each continent drafted a continental survey. The respective groups of African, Asian, Latin American, and Western bishops presented each their own synthesis at the synod.

In more ways than one, this synod marked a turning point in church history. The increasing importance of the third church became obvious. It was the first time that the bishops of the third church not only outnumbered the others, but also constituted the more dynamic and creative wing. The minority situation of the Western church also became evident. Henceforth the Third World churches would play a predominant role within the universal church. Church problems could no longer be studied without the contribution of the African, Asian, and Latin American churches. The evolution went on and manifested itself still more clearly at the 1977 and 1980 synods of bishops.

The 1974 synod considered evangelization in a broad sense, as equivalent to the overall mission of the church. In this perspective, evangelization is a responsibility to be shouldered by all the churches. It includes both pastoral and missionary (first) evangelization. For the young churches this means church upbuilding, deepening of the faith, and self-evangelization, but also the first proclamation to non-Christians, the *ad gentes* mission. The synodal discussions on *ad gentes* evangelization did not refer only to local or *ad intra* evangelization, but also to worldwide or *ad extra* evangelization. The bishops of the young churches declared that they were willing to participate in the churches' joint task of world evangelization. They want to have, as soon as possible, enough resources of their own to assume their responsibility in worldwide evangelization *ad extra*.

Nonetheless, the presence of foreign missionaries remains both desirable and needed, even if sufficient local resources are available. Their presence is a sign of the local churches' universal openness and fellowship, and it promotes solidarity and exchange between local churches. However, missionaries ought to be sent in a spirit of reciprocity. The churches of Europe, North America, and elsewhere must be ready to invite priests, religious, and lay persons to come to them and perform missionary work with them. Every church must give and receive. "The still prevailing, old and worn out 'father-son' relationship between the churches must be superseded by the relationship between older and younger brothers" (Bishop J. Sangu). Thus the African bishops. Bishop P. Kalilombe stated:

> We are ready to send Christians from among us to you. They have no money, but they will, by living among you, help you discover a new dimension of your personality, a new approach to problems, a new ecclesial feeling, a new insight into mission.

In their joint declaration at the close of the synod, the African bishops returned to this idea:

> Collegiality, co-responsibility, ecclesial communion are synonyms of the one fundamental reality: we are members of the same family; everyone individually and we all together are responsible for God's church, spread all over the world.

Cardinal Picachy (Calcutta) remarked: "India, an evangelized church, is now, in her turn, sending missionaries to all parts of the world."

The Apostolic Exhortation *Evangelii Nuntiandi* of Paul VI (Dec. 8, 1975), the fruit of the synod's reflection, is a remarkable document. According to John Paul II it may be viewed as the "Magna Charta for the work of evangelization in the last quarter of the century" (July 10, 1980). This document is a further reflection on the missionary doctrine of Vatican II. What *Ad Gentes* kept referring to as an outdated understanding of mission is not to be found in *Evangelii Nuntiandi*. There is no longer any distinction between younger and older churches. Mutual relationships are free of all forms of paternalism. Reciprocity replaces the former one-way directionality. The church's missionary character is even more emphasized than in *Ad Gentes*. "Evangelizing is in fact the church's own grace and vocation, [its] deepest identity. [It] exists in order to evangelize" (n. 14). Every community that is being evangelized must in its turn become an evangelizing community. "Those who have received the good news and who have been gathered by it into a community of salvation can and must communicate and spread it" (n. 13). "The first evangelization to those who do not yet know Christ has always been the fundamental program of the church" (n. 51).

Evangelii Nuntiandi uses the term "evangelization" in a broad sense and gradually discards the term "mission." Yet, in conformity with the synod, *Evangelii Nuntiandi* states that the church will know no rest as long as it has not tried its utmost to preach the good news (missionary evangelization). It must always continue to form new preachers:

> Let us state this fact with joy at a time when there is no lack of people who think and even say that ardor and the apostolic spirit are exhausted and that the time of the missions is now past. The synod has replied that the missionary proclamation never ceases and that the church will always be striving for the fulfillment of this proclamation [n. 53].

The text of Mark, "Go to the whole world and preach the gospel to all mankind," was the action program of the apostles and of the first Christians. This program must continue (n. 49). *Evangelii Nuntiandi* reacts against preachers who, for whatever reason, yield to the temptation of limiting their missionary activity (nn. 49–50) or give in to fatigue, disappointment, mediocrity, lack of interest, and above all lack of joy and hope (n. 80). As in *Ad Gentes*, bishops, priests, and religious are reminded of their missionary obligations.

The 1974 synod of bishops and *Evangelii Nuntiandi* found an enthusiastic response in Third World churches. These documents invite the bishops and the priests to a serious reflection on their missionary duty.

In September 1968 the Latin American Episcopal Conference (CELAM) held a meeting of decisive importance at Medellín, Colombia. Guided by Vatican II, the bishops examined church renewal in the Latin American context.

Church renewal in the Indian context was the theme of the All-India Seminar, a very important plenary meeting of the bishops' conference of India, held in 1969 in Bangalore. Like Medellín, it was a miniature Vatican II. The bishops dealt with the problem of evangelization, but taken almost exclusively in its *ad intra* dimension. It was only when preparing for the 1974 synod of bishops and afterward that Third World churches paid full attention to mission *ad extra*.

The first plenary meeting of the pan-Asiatic bishops' conference (FABC: Federation of Asian Bishops' Conferences, founded in 1970), which took place in Taipei in April 1974, discussed the theme of evangelization in Asia, in preparation for the synod of bishops. In the conclusions we read:

> Asia is beginning to send out its own missionaries. Some nations, which are older and stronger in Christianity, send priests and sisters to other Asian nations which have greater need. We feel that the day is fast approaching when Asia will send missionaries to the other continents [this was already being done at that time].

On the occasion of his visit to Manila in November 1970, Paul VI invited the Asian bishops to launch a missionary movement.

The pan-African bishops' conference (SECAM: Symposium of the Episcopal Conferences of Africa and Madagascar, founded in 1969) discussed the problem of evangelization in Africa during its fourth general assembly in Rome in September 1975. It stressed the urgency of *ad gentes* mission both *ad intra* and *ad extra*. Paul VI had already stressed the missionary vocation of the African church in his address to the African bishops at Kampala in 1969.

In Latin America as well as in Africa and Asia, bishops have held national and regional meetings to study the question of *ad extra* evangelization. Many bishops' conferences have set up an episcopal commission for the missions. CELAM has had a mission department for many years, with ramifications in diverse Latin American countries.

Reflection on evangelization has proved to be a blessing for Third World churches. Some indigenous bishops and priests had been inclined to restrict themselves to pastoral care among their own Christians, thus forming Christian ghettos in a non-Christian society and neglecting the proclamation of the good news to the non-Christians of their region. They lacked the "militant" spirit of foreign missionaries. Still another gap needed to be filled in: the young churches needed to open up to the outside world and evolve from being closed and merely receptive churches to become active, "giving" churches. They had to discover that being missionary *ad extra* is an indispensable element of Christian maturity and vitality. Sharing is a law of life.

It can be said that thanks to Vatican II and the 1974 synod of bishops, Third World bishops underwent a radical change of mentality with regard to mission. Previously, on account of the shortage of priests, it seemed inconceivable that bishops should supply personnel to go and evangelize elsewhere. When in the 1960s the C.I.C.M. Fathers planned to send Zairian members to other African countries, they met with strong opposition from indigenous bishops and priests. This should not surprise us. In former years, the same mentality had prevailed in the Western churches. When in 1911 Fr. James A. Walsh intended to found, in the U.S.A., a society of diocesan priests for foreign missions (Maryknoll), the bishops judged his initiative premature. In spite of the insistence of Pius XI (*Rerum Ecclesiae*, 1926), Pius XII (*Fidei Donum*, 1957), and John XXIII (*Princeps Pastorum*, 1959), many European bishops remained reluctant to promote missionary vocations among their own clergy. Few acceded to Pius XII when he asked that even dioceses with insufficient clergy supply priests for missionary work.

Undoubtedly, the words and deeds of Paul VI, and even more so those of John Paul II, have had a great influence on the growing missionary impulse in the Third World. Both popes became traveling missionaries and stimulated the young churches to become missionary in their turn. John Paul II's declarations are quite impressive. He reveals how much mission has become a preoccupation for him:

> The breakthrough of mission is the most obsessing and even the daily concern of my heart. My trips to the faraway countries where Christian communities still constitute a minority are, as it were, a sign of this anxiety [address of June 28, 1982].

The Rise of the Third Church

The heightening of missionary consciousness in Third World churches must be seen in the context of the "coming of the third church"—the title of a fascinating book by Walbert Bühlmann.

Numerous facts and statistics point to an important revolution that has begun within the universal church. The center of gravity within the church is moving very quickly from the Western churches to the churches of the South and the East—that is, to the third church, to the churches of the poor nations.

The history of the latest synods of bishops, where Third World bishops outnumbered the others and continued to increase their influence, confirms this assertion.

In 1960, 51 percent of all Catholics lived in Europe and North America. By the year 2000 this will be down to 30 percent only. At the turn of the next century half of the Catholic world population will live in Latin America. About that time, Africa will have almost as many Christians as will Western Europe.

According to the *Annuarium Statisticum Ecclesiae 1980* (1982 edition) there were 2,452 particular churches (ecclesiastical subdivisions: dioceses or the equivalent) at the end of 1980. Only 948 of them were in Europe and North America. This means therefore that most bishops reside in the Third World.

Of the 448 bishops (residential and titular) in Africa, about 300 are Africans (67 percent). Of the 535 bishops in Asia, about 400 are Asians (75 percent). Of the 101 bishops in Oceania, 60 are of local origin (59 percent). Of the 951 bishops in Latin America, 735 are of local origin (77 percent).

Whereas the college of cardinals had but 13 Third World members out of 80 at the 1963 conclave, 52 of the 111 members of the 1978 conclave were non-Westerners. The papal election of John Paul II demonstrated that this evolution had a bearing on the choice of a non-Italian pope. The election of a non-Western pope is no longer unthinkable.

More and more clerics from the Third World are filling important offices in departments of the Roman Curia. A large number of Third World seminarians and priests are studying at ecclesiastical universities in Rome and other First World centers. Quite a few African and Asian priests are exercising their apostolate in Europe and North America.

Maybe we are not yet sufficiently aware of the fact that the main trends of thought regarding church renewal (building of the church from the grass roots, liberation theology, respect for popular religiosity, liturgical renewal, etc.) originated in Third World churches. It is also well to point out the growing influence of Third World theology, which questions and challenges the monopoly maintained by a theology linked with Western culture.

The present membership of the superior council of the Pontifical Mission Aid Societies is a typical example of the rise of the Third World churches. In the past it was almost exclusively composed of delegates from Western donor churches. More recently, and as a consequence of the young churches' maturity, Pontifical Mission Aid Societies have been established in almost every country. Their national directors are members of the superior council in Rome and constitute a majority. They join in decisions regarding the distribution of funds. Their churches, formerly only receiving churches, are now contributing to the international solidarity fund. But the new national directors understand that, as mentioned in the new statutes of the Pontifical Mission Aid Societies, their first task consists in awakening a missionary consciousness in their local churches, rather than in collecting funds. Directors in Latin America and the Philippines have become very active in this respect.

The evolution within international religious institutes is another example of the church's internal shift from North to South and East. Here too the center of gravity is moving toward the Third World. At present many of these institutes recruit most of their candidates in Third World countries. It can be expected that in the coming years these Third World members will be very influential. Several general councils count representatives from non-Western churches. The Missionary Sisters of the Immaculate Heart of Mary (I.C.M., Heverlee, Belgium), have a Filipina superior general.

In India and Sri Lanka in 1981, the Jesuits had about 3,000 local members in 11 provinces and vice-provinces—the largest number after that of the U.S.A. With 137 novices, the novitiate in Ranchi had the highest Jesuit enrollment in the world. In 1981, the S.V.D. Fathers (Steyl) numbered 1,046 scholastics (philosophy and theology students), of whom 716 were from the Third World (Indonesia, 191; the Philippines, 159; India, 136). In 1978 they ordained 90 priests, among them 47 Asians, 3 Brazilians, 3 Argentinians, 1 African, and 1 New Zealander. In 1982, 200 of the 300 C.I.C.M. Fathers under the age of 40 were non-European.

Other religious institutes are evolving in the same direction. In some countries the missionary work of some missionary institutes has been taken over almost entirely by indigenous members—for example, in India and Vietnam. Of the 250 Capuchin Fathers working in Indonesia, 150 are Indonesians. Of the 130 Brothers of Maastricht (Holland), 100 are Indonesians (3 of them are working in Ghana). The Dutch Sisters of St. Charles Borromeo, who count about 1,000 members, have 320 Indonesian members.

Many missionary institutes have very few new candidates in their Western provinces, whereas their novitiates in the third church are doing well. Today the C.I.C.M. Fathers, for example, have but a small number of candidates in Europe and the U.S.A., but they count 30 novices in Zaire and the Philippines. The I.C.M. Sisters number 5 candidates in Belgium, as compared with 30 in India, the Philippines, and Zaire.

These facts point to the ever growing importance of the Third World churches and their missionary activity within the universal church.

The heightening of missionary consciousness in Third World churches is closely linked to the development of the religious life in those countries. Hence we need to examine in greater detail the expansion of the religious life in the third church.

First, however, I shall give some statistics on the number of priests and seminarians. This may be useful to better understand the missionary movement that is growing in Third World churches.

Church Statistics

Numbers of Priests as of 1980

- Africa: 6,052 diocesan and 11,294 religious priests. Most of the diocesan priests are Africans; the religious, except for about 400, are non-African. Thus about two-thirds of all priests are non-African. But very soon half of the clergy will be African.
- Asia: 13,555 diocesan and 13,581 religious priests. Practically all the diocesan priests, and the majority of the religious

priests, are Asians. More than two-thirds of all priests are Asians.
- Latin America: 23,281 diocesan and 25,497 religious priests. About half of all the priests are Latin Americans.
- Oceania: 2,912 diocesan and 2,755 religious priests.
- Europe: 168,908 diocesan and 74,411 religious priests (Poland: 15,157 and 4,358, respectively; Italy: 40,649 and 23,080).
- North America: 42,701 diocesan and 28,653 religious priests.

All told, there are 413,600 priests (diocesan and religious), of whom 98,927 reside in the third church (24 percent).

During the period from 1975 to 1980, the numbers of priests evolved as follows: Europe, 4.6 percent decrease; North America, 0.5 percent decrease; Africa, 19 percent increase; Asia, 11.5 percent increase; Central America, 1.6 percent increase; South America, 1.8 percent increase; Oceania, 1 percent decrease. The regression in the Western world has been continuing since that time, as has also the increase in the Third World.

Priestly Ordinations (Diocesan), 1980 Compared with 1975

- Africa: 397 (284 in 1975).
- Asia: 562 (447 in 1975).
- Latin America: 528 (536 in 1975).
- Oceania: 43 (71 in 1975).
- Europe: 1,682 (1,966 in 1975).
- North America: 648 (835 in 1975).

In 1980 there were 1,530 ordinations in the third church and 2,330 in the Western churches; in 1975 there were 1,338 and 2,801, respectively. Thus, more than a third of all newly ordained priests come from the third church. The number of major seminarians reveals how quickly the moment is approaching when there will be more ordinations in the Third World than in the First.

Major Seminarians, 1980 Compared with 1975

- Africa: 5,448 diocesan and 1,101 religious (in 1975: 3,883 and 512, respectively).

- Asia: 7,421 diocesan and 4,769 religious (in 1975: 6,343 and 3,971).
- Latin America: 8,896 diocesan and 5,261 religious (in 1975: 5,842 and 3,878).
- Oceania: 526 diocesan and 411 religious (in 1975: 573 and 446).
- Europe: 16,438 diocesan and 7,228 religious (in 1975: 15,960 and 8,223) [Poland, diocesan and religious, 6,101; Italy, 5,076].
- North America: 5,414 diocesan and 3,129 religious (in 1975: 6,446 and 4,065).

This yields as totals: 33,833 in the Third World and 32,209 in the First. In fact the number of seminarians in the third church is larger still: we lack statistics for Vietnam and China. We may safely say that the third church will have the majority of future priests. These statistics date back to the end of 1980. Since then the number of major seminarians in Africa, Asia, and Latin America has continued to grow.

Distribution of Priests throughout the World

A document issued by the Congregation for the Clergy (March 25, 1980), "Norms for the Cooperation of Local Churches among Themselves and Especially for a Better Distribution of the Clergy in the World," gives the following data: for every 100,000 Catholics there are 16 priests in Latin America, 33 in Africa, 43 in South and East Asia, 93 in Europe, 120 in North America. This means that in Latin America there are 6,250 Catholics for every priest; in Africa, 3,030; for the whole of Asia, 2,213; in Europe, 1,075; and in North America, 833.

For every 100,000 persons there are 2 priests in Asia, 4 in Africa, 13 in Latin America, 26 in Oceania, 29 in North America, 31 in Europe.

Europe and North America, which account for 45 percent of the Catholic world population, have 77 percent of all the priests. Latin America and the Philippines, which also account for 45 percent of the Catholic world population, have but 12.6 percent of all the priests. The shortage of priests is the sharpest in Latin

America and the Philippines (in the Philippines there is but one priest for every 7,776 Catholics).

Expansion of the Religious Life in Africa, Asia, and Oceania

Whereas the number of candidates for the religious life is alarmingly regressive in the Western churches (except in Poland and Ireland), Africa and Asia are witnessing a true explosion of religious vocations. In terms of absolute numbers, there are still fewer religious in the young churches than in the Western churches. To be sure, the expansion of religious life can start only when a young church has reached a certain maturity. Expansion started later in Africa than in Asia; the African church is a few centuries younger than the Asian.

At the end of 1980 the entire church counted 229,281 religious men (156,191 priests and 73,090 nonpriests). The number of religious priests in the Third World churches has already been mentioned. So far, there are still very few religious priests in Africa. Until about 1970 the Congregation de Propaganda Fide (Sacred Congregation for the Evangelization of the Peoples) and the bishops promoted the diocesan clergy by discouraging the expansion of clerical religious life. Whether this was a wise policy is debatable. The normal proportion between diocesan and religious clergy is 65 (diocesan) to 35 (religious). This proportion is verified in Asia.

The explosion of religious life prevails foremost among African and Asian religious women. Worldwide there are 960,991 religious women:

- Africa: 35,586, of whom 14,000 are Africans.
- Asia: 87,889, of whom more than 76,000 are Asians (in India alone there are approx. 49,500).
- Oceania: 16,072.
- Latin America: 125,280.
- Europe: 527,707.
- North America: 168,457.

Thus, there are 264,827 sisters (including expatriates) in the third church.

It is only recently that Africa and Asia have experienced an explosion of religious life, of both men and women. The impressive number of young religious has already been mentioned. We have not any information about the numbers of novices, men and women, in Western religious institutes. But everybody knows that they are alarmingly low. We know the numbers of African and Asian novices quite well. For some years now the Pontifical Mission Aid Societies have been granting an annual subsidy (approx. $250) for every autochthonous first-year novice in Africa, Asia, and Oceania. The religious institutes there do not fail to communicate the numbers of their novices.

In 1980 there were about 2,000 African and Asian first-year novices (clerical and other) in the religious institutes for men. Some novitiates in Africa and Asia are filled to capacity. The following figures refer to first-year novices. The Apostles of Jesus had 36 novices in their novitiate in Kenya and 32 in their novitiate in Uganda. The C.I.C.M. Fathers had 20 in their novitiate in Kinshasa; the Holy Spirit Fathers had 14 in their novitiate in Nigeria and 10 in their novitiate in Tanzania. India especially has very many young candidates. The 10 Jesuit novitiates together counted 137 members; the Salesian Fathers had 114 candidates in their four novitiates (46 in their novitiate in Ootacamund); the Carmelites of Mary Immaculate (Syro-Malabar) have 61 candidates in five novitiates in Kerala.

The number of women novices is larger still than that of men and can be estimated at about 5,000. Novitiates with 20 or 30 first-year novices are not unusual, in Africa as well as Asia. In 1980 the Sisters of the Immaculate Heart of Mary in Onitsha (Nigeria) had 41 novices; the Evangelizing Sisters of Mary (Moshi, Tanzania) had 24; the Our Lady of Kilimanjaro Sisters (Moshi), 22; the Daughters of Charity (Tabora, Tanzania), 41. In Asia, especially in India and the Philippines, there are several novitiates with comparable enrollments. In Zaire there are at present 50 congregations for religious women—indigenous and expatriate. The large number of novitiates explains why, in general, they have smaller enrollments. The Priory of the Resurrection (canonesses, Bukavu), founded in 1966, already counts 99 professed sisters and has about 100 novices and postulants.

Institutional Commitment to Mission

Africa and Asia count a great number of indigenous congregations for women, mostly diocesan congregations. The number of indigenous congregations of brothers is also very impressive. Rather few, however, are the indigenous clerical congregations. There are several in India but only one in Africa. Almost all local clerical religious belong to Western orders, congregations, and societies. International religious institutes, of both men and women, recruit local candidates. As mentioned before, the mission provinces of many of these institutes already have more indigenous members than foreign members. That is, most of the more specifically missionary institutes started the process of indigenization some years ago—for example, the S.V.D. Fathers, the C.I.C.M. Fathers, the Combonian Fathers (Verona), the Xaverian Fathers (Parma), the Missionaries of Consolata (Turin), the Franciscan Missionaries of Mary, the I.C.M. Sisters (Heverlee). Some missionary societies without vows, especially those with strong national ties, do not recruit locally—for example, the Foreign Missions of Paris, the Bethlehem Missionaries (Switzerland), and the Maryknoll Missionaries (U.S.A.). In their understanding, their task consists only in assisting a local church until it has sufficient resources of its own. Once this is achieved, their mission is accomplished.

The missionary institutes that recruit local members are convinced that they are rendering a service to the local church by helping it to become missionary *ad extra*. It is invited to profit from their many years of experience in the field of evangelization and from a well-organized missionary involvement. They do not help in view of increasing their own chances of survival. These considerations stimulated some missionary institutes, formerly reluctant to accept local candidates, to start recruiting in the local church. So, for example, the White Fathers and the White Sisters. The latter had first helped to found 20 African religious congregations. In 1977 the White Fathers decided to recruit African members for their society. They now have training houses in Ghana, Uganda, Tanzania, and Zaire.

Most missionaries sent out by Third World churches have belonged to international congregations. Consequently, their spreading brought with it a universal character. A bond is thus established between the young churches and the churches of other countries and continents. Indian Jesuits are working in all continents. Philippine C.I.C.M. Fathers and I.C.M. Sisters are working in other Asian countries and in Africa and Latin America. Oblate Fathers from Sri Lanka perform missionary work in India, Pakistan, and Malaysia. The multinational membership of international missionary institutes enables them to send out international teams of missionaries.

Institutionally organized missionary involvement offers many advantages. Mission history of the past few centuries teaches that evangelization has been almost exclusively an undertaking of religious or missionary societies without vows. Mission work *ad extra*, especially pioneering work, makes great demands with regard to training, as well as spiritual and material assistance. Hence it is preferable that it be done through the mediation of an institute. Thus we read in *Ad Gentes*:

> Since experience teaches too that mission work itself cannot be accomplished by lone individuals, a common calling has gathered individuals together into communities. In these, thanks to united efforts, they can be properly trained and will be able to carry out this work in the name of the church and according to hierarchy directives [n. 27].

Such an institutional commitment is more advisable for Third World churches than it is for churches of the West. At least for the time being, Third World churches can hardly meet the requirements of training and accompaniment. As we shall see, some Asian and African episcopal conferences have taken the initiative of setting up a mission seminary or a missionary society for diocesan priests. These foundations knew but little success. This will probably not change, unless such foundations evolve toward autonomous institutes, with or without vows.

This does not mean, however, that the exchange of diocesan priests between dioceses or the sending of Fidei Donum priests should be underestimated. Pius XII, in his encyclical *Fidei Donum* (1957), as well as his successors and Vatican II (A.G. n. 38), urged the bishops to yield some of their own priests to dioceses short of priests in other countries or continents.

In 1977 there were about 2,000 Fidei Donum priests. By means of this formula bishops give a direct witness of their sense of missionary responsibility, and interchurch solidarity is expressed in a tangible way. But priests sent out this way will always remain few in numbers, due to the problems connected with this kind of missionary involvement. The difficulties inherent in this system are more serious for priests of Third World churches than they are for those of First World churches.

Third World episcopal conferences have repeatedly discussed the problem of lending priests to dioceses short of priests. In fact, due to many local circumstances, the number of priests available in one diocese is sometimes very different from that in other dioceses of the same country or neighboring countries. No matter how much bishops intend to help one another, their plans usually know but little success. To solve the shortage of priests, it is much easier to call upon religious priests: not being tied to a particular diocese, they can more easily move from one to another.

As in the time of the Western missionary expansion, so also now in the Third World churches, *ad extra* mission will largely remain the work of religious. Vatican II stressed the missionary nature of the religious life (L.G. n. 44; A.G. n. 40; P.C. n. 20). *Evangelii Nuntiandi* says:

> Religious find in their consecrated life a privileged means of effective evangelization, and continue to bring an immense contribution to evangelization. . . . Thanks to their consecration they are eminently willing and free to leave everything and to go and proclaim the gospel even to the ends of the earth. They are enterprising and their apostolate is often marked by an originality, by a genius that calls forth admiration. They are generous; often they are found at the outposts of the mission, and they take the greatest risks for their health, and their very lives. Truly the church owes them much [n. 69].

But to remain faithful to the spirit of Vatican II, religious institutes must, more than ever before, work in close cooperation with local churches. Only then will local churches be able to consider religious missionaries their own missionaries, incorporated into the local people of God.

CHAPTER TWO

THE RISE OF MISSIONARY CONSCIOUSNESS IN AFRICA

General Survey

The young church of Africa is confronted with many serious problems in an independent, but interiorly torn and economically undermined Africa. Yet that church is full of dynamism and promise. It is becoming an important and increasingly creative wing within the universal church. African Christianity (Catholicism, Protestantism, independent churches) has enjoyed a spectacular growth in recent decades. The increase in numbers of Christians (through births and conversions) exceeds 7 million a year, including more than 2 million Catholics. The number of Catholics tripled between 1950 and 1970. At the end of 1980 there were 58,676,000 Catholics. If we add catechumens and aspirants, the figure amounts to about 70 million. Baptized Catholics represent 12.5 percent of the total African population (469,543,000) or 15 percent if we consider sub-Saharan Africa only. In spite of the tenacity of Islam, sociologists predict that by the end of the century Africa will be more than 50 percent Christian and that it will count almost as many Christians as will Europe, and more than will the United States. According to D. Barrett, 18 percent of all Christians will reside in Africa.

North Africa forms a Muslim bloc with but very few Catholics. In some countries of sub-Saharan Africa the percentage of Catholics is also quite small—for example, in the Muslim regions. In some other countries Catholics amount to about 50 percent of the national population—for example, Burundi, Rwanda, Gabon, Zaire. In Kinshasa, 58 percent of the 2.8 million inhabitants are Catholic, 27 percent are Protestant, and 10 percent are Kimbanguist. Kinshasa can be considered one of the world's most Christian cities.

In previous years, it seemed that this spectacular growth would create a frightening problem for the Catholic Church, because of the ever greater shortage of priests. Whereas the number of foreign missionaries went on diminishing, the increase of indigenous priests did not follow the growth rate of the faithful. Hence the problem: How can the church of Africa acquire sufficient pastoral workers to ensure the spiritual care of the ever increasing number of believers? In 1980 there was but one African priest for every 9,000 Catholics. But the perspectives have become less alarming. The spirit of God has provoked a surprising evolution within the church, which sociologists could not foresee. Several countries have witnessed a true vocation explosion, and there has been an enormous involvement of lay persons in numerous basic communities.

It is in the light of these data that we must appraise the growing missionary movement in Africa. In spite of its own huge problems, Africa is becoming a missionary continent.

The Vatican II ecclesiology, the 1974 synod of bishops, and *Evangelii Nuntiandi* contributed a great deal to the awakening of a missionary consciousness among African bishops, priests, and religious. The living witness of many foreign missionaries helped many young persons to discover the specifically missionary vocation. Paul VI's famous and prophetic words pronounced at Kampala (1969) were very stimulating:

> By now, you Africans are missionaries to yourselves. . . . To the impulse given to the faith by the missionary action of foreign countries, and consequent upon it, there must now be associated an impulse arising from the heart of Africa itself. The church is, by [its] very nature, always a missionary church.

The pope added that the presence of foreign missionaries remains as absolute necessity. His words met with an enthusiastic response in Africa. Even today, they are still frequently quoted.

The African church has undergone, as we know, an interior revolution. Thanks to the numerous small Christian communities, the church is developing from the grass roots; its work is increasingly borne by the people. The vocation explosion is mainly due to the intense faith and dynamism of the basic Christian communities. They created the suitable climate for a spontaneous burgeoning of vocations. These communities are more and more open and outgoing. The universal dimension of the church, communion with other churches, and evangelization *ad extra* all appeal to them.

On the occasion of his first visit to Africa, John Paul II did not fail to stimulate the awakening missionary spirit. He did so in his address to the bishops' conference of Zaire (Kinshasa, May 3, 1980), Ghana (Kumasi, May 9, 1980), and the Ivory Coast (Abidjan, May 11, 1980). He recalled the famous words of Paul VI. He said that the collaboration of foreign missionaries was still indispensable to make up for the shortage of personnel, to witness to the universality of the church, and to promote interchurch exchange. He said that Paul VI's words, "You are now your own missionaries," have partially come true already—that is, regarding evangelization *ad intra* largely carried on by indigenous personnel. He added, however, that today evangelization must also develop an *ad extra* dimension. In his address to the bishops of Zaire we read:

> "You are now your own missionaries," Paul VI said in Kampala eleven years ago. That has been in part realized. But to this I want to add : aim to be missionaries in your turn, not only in this country where many are still waiting for the proclamation of the gospel, but outside, and in particular in other African countries. A church that gives, even of its limited resources, will be blessed by the Lord, for one always finds somebody poorer than oneself.

Having spoken of the promotion of priestly and religious vocations, the pope told the bishops of Ghana:

I wish to reflect on another dimension: the missionary responsibility of your churches for the needs of sister churches in Africa and elsewhere. I understand your worries concerning the needs of your own Christian communities, which must be animated by priests chosen by God, from among your own people. However, let us not forget that God will never delay to bless those who give generously. The promotion of missionary vocations—whether according to the formula proposed by Fidei Donum, or by joining an international mission society—will move the local community to greater confidence in God's grace and a deepening faith consciousness.

For a church to be missionary, it is not enough to send out some missionaries. The people of God as a whole must become missionary:

> It is your whole church that must become missionary: priests, religious, lay persons, and also the communities themselves, by their openness, their witness, and their explicit proclamation among those who still do not know the gospel. This they must do in their own country and in the other African countries [to the bishops of the Ivory Coast, May 11, 1980].

Pope John Paul II's allocutions on his second African visit reveal once more his great concern for the deepening of missionary consciousness in Africa. At Lagos, on February 11, 1982, he expressed his appreciation of African missionary undertakings:

> I rejoice deeply that you have begun to send missionaries to other lands, even before you have laborers enough for your own vineyard. I am happy to know that you have Nigerian priests in Sierra Leone, Liberia, the People's Republic of the Congo, Zambia and, still further afield, in Grenada. There is a Nigerian brother in Kenya. And there are sisters in Ghana, Sierra Leone, Liberia, Gabon, Angola, Kenya, and Zambia; sisters are serving also in Turin. Another visible sign of your desire to hand on the faith is the establishment in 1977 of your national missionary seminary.

A missionary Africa is a dream that John Paul II will not relinquish. At Cotonou, Benin, he reiterated his missionary appeal in his homily on February 17, 1982:

> Thank God, if foreign missionaries are still a precious help to you. Yet, it is more and more the duty of the people of Benin, especially of the priests and religious, to go from diocese to diocese and proclaim the good news to the people of Benin, and . . . even to other African peoples beyond your own borders [Cotonou, Feb. 17, 1982].

The African bishops, who previously were reluctant to promote vocations for foreign religious institutes, are now much more obliging in this respect. Those of English-speaking East Africa openly support the promotion of missionary vocations. They no longer consider the promotion of vocations to the religious life as harmful to their own vocational promotion. Several countries have experienced an explosion of vocations: Zaire, Uganda, Tanzania, Kenya, Nigeria, and others. Several major seminaries are being built because the existing ones are too small. The Bigard Memorial Seminary (Enugu, Nigeria) enrolled about 350 major seminarians for the academic year 1980–1981. In August 1981, 69 new priests were ordained. Rooms were lacking to admit some of the 104 new candidates for the academic year 1981–1982.

Episcopal conferences have created their own commissions on mission, which pay more and more attention to evangelization *ad extra*. The bishops of Burundi are proud that Burundese priests and sisters are working in Tanzania, Zaire, Rwanda, Uganda, Chad, and Cameroon. Since 1972 the Benetereziya Sisters have been working in Chad, where they have two communities and are helping with the foundation of a local religious congregation. Bishop Ruhuna (Gitega), chairman of the Burundese commission on mission, says that "if we do not give, we shall not receive; the church is like the heart that gives and receives life."

Pope John Paul II praised the Nigerian bishops who lend priests to other dioceses short of priests, whether in Nigeria or elsewhere. The bishops of Tanzania are doing the same thing.

The diocese of Moshi, Tanzania, can be taken as a model of a missionary diocese (in the active sense). Half of its total population (400,000) is Catholic. Of its 110 priests, 103 are African. Due to the large number of Catholics, it suffers from an acute shortage of priests. This does not prevent the bishop from supporting the missionary movement of his diocese. About twenty of his priests are working in other dioceses of Tanzania and in Kenya. Thirteen priests belong to missionary institutes and are working in other countries. The African missionary congregation, the Apostles of Jesus, enjoys the bishop's full support. Some diocesan priests and major seminarians, besides many young laymen, have joined this congregation. The Apostles of Jesus have a minor seminary in Uru. The women's branch of this congregation, the Evangelizing Sisters of Mary, was founded in 1977 and opened its first novitiate in the diocese of Moshi. In the same diocese, the Capuchin Fathers have a minor seminary with 118 students. Here also, upon request of the Conference of Tanzanian Major Religious Superiors, the Capuchin Fathers started a training course for religious missionaries. The famous congregation of the Sisters of Our Lady of Kilimanjaro, founded in the diocese of Moshi, has its central house there. Today the sisters are working in various dioceses of Tanzania and in Kenya.

The bishops of Nigeria have also given evidence of their mission-mindedness. On the insistent requests of Cardinal Ekandem (Ikot Ekpene), the episcopal conference decided in 1976 to open a mission seminary at Iperu (diocese of Ijebu-Ode). By so doing the bishops responded to the appeal of Vatican II (A. G. n. 20) and of Paul VI. This seminary is training priests who will be sent to dioceses in need of priests in Nigeria or in other countries. In 1982 the seminary had 62 candidates from 17 dioceses. Established as a *pia societas* in 1979, under the name of Missionary Society of St. Paul, it seems to be evolving toward the status of a missionary institute.

African Religious in the Service of Mission

In the past, the bishops objected to the promotion of the clerical religious life. More recently, however, their attitude has changed. This has been beneficial to the development of the religious life, as well as to the growing missionary movement. Most religious institutes—both the exclusively missionary and the others—that are involved in missionary work in Africa and have opened novitiates can boast of important and ever growing numbers of candidates. The number of African members of the various monastic foundations also continues to increase.

Religious institutes that are not exclusively missionary also pursue missionary work in diverse African countries. Their African candidates are often sent *ad extra* and consequently they are given missionary training. The exclusively missionary institutes stipulate that readiness for service *ad extra* is a requirement for admission to the institute.

In Zaire, 24 clerical religious institutes (all of foreign origin) recruit members. In 1980 they counted 113 novices in all (the C.I.C.M. Fathers, 20; the Oblates, 16; the Jesuits, 15; the Norbertines, 9; the Salesians, 5). They had 146 students of philosophy (the C.I.C.M. Fathers, 31; the Oblates, 22; the White Fathers, 17; the Jesuits, 16; the Salesians, 10) and 60 students of theology (the C.I.C.M. Fathers, 17; the Salesians, 10; the Jesuits, 8).

The foreign and indigenous congregations of brothers also have many vocations in Zaire. The impressive number of major (diocesan) seminarians in 1981—1,377 (200 more than the year before)—is worth mentioning.

In Nigeria, especially in the southern dioceses, the vocation explosion is even greater than in Zaire. In 1981 there were 679 diocesan priests and 1,003 major seminarians (in five seminaries). The number of indigenous priests is considerably higher than that of foreign priests. In 1979 the seven clerical religious institutes counted a total of 68 novices and 150 scholastics (Holy Spirit Fathers, 60; Claretians, 36; Lazarists, 15; Dominicans, 9; Augustinians, 6; Benedictines, 22 Cistercians, 2).

At present the Jesuit African assistency has two provinces and three vice-provinces in Africa. Already one-fourth of the members are African and Malagasy. In 1982 they had 94 priests, 84 brothers, 28 scholastics, and 59 novices (in 6 novitiates). The majority of their members come from Central Africa (109) and Madagascar (100). The most renowned novitiate is that of Central Africa, at Cyangugu in Rwanda (39 novices).

African priests and brothers belonging to religious institutes in Zaire, Nigeria, and elsewhere perform mission work in several African countries and even outside Africa. Nigerian and Tanzanian Holy Spirit Fathers work in Zambia; Nigerian Holy Spirit Fathers in Gambia and in the Congo Republic. Aside from Zaire itself, Zairian C.I.C.M. Fathers are also in Cameroon, Zambia, Nigeria, and Brazil. Haiti and the black population of the United States are also on their program. Mauritius has 22 priests, mostly religious, working abroad—in Madagascar, Réunion, South Africa, Brazil, Taiwan, and elsewhere.

Does it serve the interests of the African church that most religious institutes working in Africa establish themselves there? This could hinder the foundation and growth of original African institutes, and interfere with the africanization of the religious life. To be sure, international institutes are better suited to localization than are the often small Western diocesan congregations. Yet the mere fact that candidates apply for admission does not justify the opening of a novitiate.

In Africa the religious life developed earlier for women than for men. Consequently, there are more religious women than men. Their number can be estimated at about 14,000. Soon it will exceed that of expatriate sisters. Most sisters belong to indigenous, mostly diocesan, congregations. Some congregations already have very many members. African sisters are more involved in pastoral work than are sisters in the West. Various training centers have been built to prepare them for this task. More and more, we see African sisters planning national and international meetings to reflect on the African expression of the religious life, on its integration into the reality of Africa, and on their task in Africa and elsewhere. The African Franciscan Missionaries of Mary from twelve different countries met in Diebougou (Upper Volta), August 18 to 24, 1981, to discuss these problems. It was their fourth meeting of this kind. Many African sisters are developing a strong missionary spirit, for *ad intra* and *ad extra* evangelization.

The Our Lady of Kilimanjaro Sisters (Moshi, founded in 1930) have 580 professed members, 57 novices (in both years of a two-year novitiate), and 30 postulants. In 1981 they had 26 newly professed members. They work in 8 dioceses of Tanzania and in 2 of Kenya. The Handmaids of the Child Jesus, founded in Calabar (Nigeria) in 1931, have 233 members and 84 novices in their two-year novitiate in Ikot Ekpene. The congregation also works abroad. Other important congregations are the Benetereziya (Burundi, founded in 1931), 400 members; the Benebikira (Rwanda, founded in 1919), 400 members; the Bannabikira (Uganda, founded in 1909), 700 members. The Sisters of the Immaculate Heart of Mary (Onitsha, founded in 1937) have 362 members and are also working outside Nigeria—in Sierra Leone, Ghana, and Kenya. They even administer a home for the elderly in Turin.

Obviously a great missionary potential is maturing in these flourishing African religious congregations for women.

The countries of the AMECEA (Association of Member Episcopal Conferences of Eastern Africa)—Kenya, Malawi, Uganda, Tanzania, Zambia, and, more recently, Ethiopia and Sudan—have the greatest concentration of priestly and religious vocations, for both men and women. Uganda and Tanzania take the lead. Here are some combined statistics (1981) for the first five countries mentioned above:

- of the 62,146,900 inhabitants, 15,041,351 are Catholic (in 70 dioceses)—that is, 24 percent;
- of the 70 residential bishops, 57 are African;
- almost half of the 4,201 priests are African; there are 1,902 African diocesan priests and about 100 African religious priests;
- there are 1,835 major (diocesan) seminarians;
- of the 1,072 brothers, 599 are African;
- of the 9,011 sisters, 6,525 are African—that is, 72 percent.

The AMECEA countries are rich in vocations. No wonder that a missionary consciousness is now very much alive there. Proof thereof is the foundation of the Apostles of Jesus, to which we now turn.

The Congregation of the Apostles of Jesus

Even though founded by foreign missionaries (the Combonian Fathers of Verona), the Apostles of Jesus is a genuinely African congregation—something unique to date. It enjoyed a tremendous development in a very short time. The founders,

Bishop S. Mazzoldi (later, bishop of Moroto, Uganda) and Father G. Marengoni, together with other missionaries, had been expelled from the Sudan. They understood well the need to train African missionaries in order to ensure the future of Christian mission. The congregation was founded in 1968 to proclaim the gospel to non-Christians and to conduct pastoral work in needy mission churches. The congregation has both priests and brothers. Members are trained to be sent to other countries of Africa or to other continents.

The first house was opened in Nadiket (diocese of Moroto) in 1969. The unexpected success of the foundation proves that the missionary ideal speaks to the desire of a growing number of African youth. Two years later, the congregation counted 142 aspirants from six countries. Not only lay persons, but also major seminarians and diocesan priests applied for admission.

By 1981 the congregation had two novitiates: one in Nadiket and one in Langata-Nairobi, Kenya. Both two-year novitiates together had 120 novices. Five minor seminaries had been opened: the first (1970) in Alokolam, Uganda; the second (1972) in Uru (diocese of Moshi) upon request of the Tanzanian bishops; the third (1973) at the request of the bishop of Bukinda, Uganda; the fourth (1974) in Kiserian near Nairobi, at the request of Cardinal Otunga; the fifth (1981) in Rejaf, Sudan. The 600 students come from Uganda, Tanzania, Kenya, Sudan, Rwanda, and Burundi. It is remarkable how enthusiastically the bishops are giving their full support to this religious congregation.

Seminaries for philosophical studies were opened at Moroto and at Langata, near Nairobi. Together they have 150 students. At the suggestion of Cardinal Otunga, the house for theological studies (with 72 students) was built in the same locality. The theology students attend classes at the Nairobi major seminary. The first two ordinations took place in June 1980; the next year there were ten.

As of 1981, Fr. Marengoni was still superior general. His four councilors are Africans, two of them novice masters and the other two rectors of a minor seminary.

On account of its rapid expansion the congregation was in need not only of financial aid, but especially of personnel for training and counseling. These tasks have been confided to 15

Combonian Fathers, assisted by religious, men and women, of other institutes. They will gradually be replaced by African members.

The constitution of the congregation borrows many elements from the constitution of the Combonian Fathers. Like the Combonian Fathers, the Apostles of Jesus intend to become an exclusively missionary congregation. Their training stresses prayer, the spirit of poverty, and pastoral aptitude. From the very start the congregation had an international character: young men from various countries and thirty tribal strains had to fraternize, which is not easy in Africa.

The congregation wants to become self-sufficient as soon as possible. All students must contribute to their upkeep by manual work. With regard to evangelization, priority is given to the poor and to pioneering work.

The congregation's option for *ad gentes* mission and its commitment to other continents might still need more clarification. The question can be raised whether the congregation is sufficiently integrated in African culture and sufficiently freed from Italian influence. In August 1981 the Combonian Fathers met at Nairobi to examine the problem of the training of African missionaries.

The Evangelizing Sisters of Mary

The congregation of the Evangelizing Sisters of Mary, the women's counterpart of the Apostles of Jesus, was founded in 1977. Some time before, fourteen women had come to see the pastor of Moshi, a member of the Apostles of Jesus, and asked him whether they too, like the men, could become missionaries and work among the poor and the neglected. With the approval of Rome a novitiate was opened at Himo (diocese of Moshi). Three training houses have already been established, in Uganda, Tanzania, and Kenya. Together they have 200 candidates. The Ongata Rongai training house (Kenya) is an approved secondary school. First vows were taken by 20 novices in 1979, and by 16 more in 1980. That same year 24 new candidates joined the congregation. The Sisters of Verona *(Pie Madri della Nigrizia)* help the congregation.

CHAPTER THREE

THE RISE OF MISSIONARY CONSCIOUSNESS IN ASIA

General Survey

According to 1981 estimates, 59 percent of the world population lives in Asia—25 percent in China and 15 percent in India. At the turn of the next century, 65 percent of the human race will be Asian (at present, 50 percent of all Asians are under 20 years of age). Asia is gradually becoming the center of the world. Next century, the destiny of Christianity will essentially be decided in Asia. And it is precisely there that Christianity is so insignificant, notwithstanding four centuries of intense evangelization. The Philippine Republic, thanks to the fact that it once was a Spanish colony, is the only Christian nation in Asia. Excluding the Philippines, Asia is less than 1 percent Catholic; with the Philippines, it is 2.4 percent Catholic. Of the 62.7 million Asian Catholics, 40.5 million live in the Philippines.

Asia is a continent rich in non-Christian cultures. It is the homeland of three eminent world religions: Islam, Buddhism, and Hinduism.

The evangelization of Asia remains an immense task. In the past, mission was essentially the work of foreign missionaries. Today it is mainly in the hands of Asian personnel. Indigenization has progressed further in Asia than in Africa. The Asian churches maintain that today the evangelization of Asia is a task for which they are themselves responsible. But at the same time, there is a growing consciousness of their responsibility for world evangelization. More than ever before, they are talking about *ad extra* mission.

The Asian churches began *ad extra* evangelization earlier than did the African churches. This is not surprising: on the one hand, their own evangelization started several centuries earlier, and on the other hand they have many more resources at their disposal. Hence we can foresee that Asia will become the most important missionary continent of the third church.

The founding of the Federation of Asian Bishops' Conferences at Manila on the occasion of Paul VI's visit in 1970 was a very important event. It became obvious that the Asian church intends to affirm its identity as a typically Asian church and that it is looking for methods apposite to the Asian context. The first general assembly of the FABC, in Taipei, April 22 to 27, 1974, expressed this very plainly. The priorities for a new missionary strategy were clearly stated: evangelization must go hand in hand with inculturation, interreligious dialogue, involvement for justice, and hence with the option for the poor. The Asian churches are taking the evangelization of Asia in their own hands, even though they continue to count on the help of foreign missionaries.

They also mentioned the problem of mission *ad extra*. In the conclusions of the meeting we read:

> Today, in most of our Asian lands the need continues for missionaries who come from other local churches. We welcome them from other countries into ours, asking only that they make themselves truly part of the local church and truly one with the people. More and more we trust our own local churches can send some of our best sons and daughters to serve our sister churches in Asia and in other continents as well [n. 39].

In spite of the immense task that awaits them, the bishops are very hopeful and optimistic about the future of the gospel in Asia. Asia is very badly in need of the gospel to solve its many religious, cultural, and economic problems. Referring to the interventions of the Asian bishops at the 1974 synod of bishops, Bishop M. Gaviola (Manila), secretary of the FABC, stated:

> You will not find among them a spirit of pessimism or defeatism, nothing of that fearful "loss of nerve" that is sometimes met today among Christians in some parts of the world. Instead you will find that they are men who have a profound conviction that the gospel of Jesus Christ and his Body which is the church belong to the future of their peoples, belong to the future of Asia. . . . Perhaps this optimism and hope, this great and joyous confidence in the saving word of Jesus Christ, is something of a contribution we from Asia, from our corner of the Third World, can bring to the church universal in this day and age, when it seems to so many, even among Christians, that the good news is neither news, nor good.

The themes that the FABC discussed in Taipei were further analyzed during regional meetings held in Seoul (Sept. 22 to 25, 1976) and Tokyo (March 26 to 29, 1979).

The FABC has three separate departments to investigate the priorities of Asian evangelization strategy: BISA (Bishops' Institute for Social Action); BIRA (Bishops' Institute for Interreligious Affairs); BIMA (Bishops' Institute for the Missionary Apostolate). The bishop members of BIMA have met with their experts to pursue their reflection on evangelization in Asia, first in Baguio (Philippines, July 12 to 17, 1978), in Ponmudi (India, Nov. 20 to 30, 1980), and in Chaghua (Taiwan, Aug. 1982). They have insisted that Asia must evangelize itself in its own way, but at the same time it must also be concerned about *ad extra* evangelization. The third BIMA meeting, attended by 26 bishops, 24 priests and religious, and 5 lay persons, stressed the missionary responsibility of the laity. The evangelization of Asia is impossible without the participation of the laity.

In his address to the Asian bishops in Manila (Nov. 28, 1970), Paul VI referred to the Asian churches' own missionary responsibility. "None better than an Asian can speak to an Asian," he said, and he added:

Your individual churches would certainly lack an essential aspect of maturity if missionary vocations did not develop within them. It is up to the bishops of Asia, up to their priests, their religious brothers and sisters and the lay people engaged in the apostolate to be the first apostles of their Asian brothers.

Proof of growing missionary consciousness in several countries is the increased attention paid to the celebration of World Mission Sunday. October becomes a period of missionary information and conscientization. In 1981 the bishops of Taiwan and Hong Kong issued a pastoral letter regarding this matter.

The religious institutes of Asia, like those of Africa, are the principal instruments for missionary involvement. As mentioned earlier, two-thirds of the religious priests are Asian (13,581), as is also the majority (86 percent) of the 87,889 sisters (i.e., 76,000). The countries with the largest number of indigenous sisters are, as of the end of 1980: India, about 49,500 (out of 50,936); the Philippines, 6,855 (out of 8,069); Korea, 3,000 (out of 3,165); Japan, 6,026 (out of 7,258); Indonesia, 2,801 (out of 4,118); Vietnam, approximately 6,000.

There are regular meetings of Asian male religious, as well as of the Asian Conference of Major Religious Superiors, attended by both men and women. Since 1972, religious women have held their own pan-Asiatic meetings, under the auspices of AMOR (Asian Meeting of Religious), in Hong Kong (1972), Manila (1974), Kyoto (1975), Bombay (1977), and Colombo (1980). All of these meetings dealt with the integration of religious life in the Asian cultural and socio-economic context. With regard to evangelization, the religious are taking the same options chosen by the bishops. They intend to be the vanguard of a praying, contemplative, and socially committed church. India is leading in this respect.

The Philippines

At the beginning of the century the church of the Philippines was powerless and seemingly moribund. Thanks to the dedication of numerous missionaries, it has recovered in less than a century and has become a flourishing and dynamic church, with numerous indigenous forces at its disposal. On account of the large number of Catholics, the shortage of priests in the Philippines is still one of the most severe in the world. But it has not prevented the Philippine church from evolving from a mission church (in the passive sense) to an evangelizing church.

With its 40.5 million Catholics out of a population of 48.4 million inhabitants, the Philippines forms an impressive Catholic front in the Asian continent. In terms of numbers—64.5 percent of all Asian Catholics—the Philippines has the sixth largest Catholic population in the world.

Among the 56 residential and 46 titular bishops, 85 are Filipinos (including 2 cardinals). There are 65 dioceses (ecclesiastical territories), 2,763 diocesan priests, most of them indigenous, and 2,201 religious priests, most of them indigenous. All told, more than 75 percent of the priests are Filipinos. Of the 8,069 sisters, 6,855 are Filipinas (85 percent). The number of major seminarians, still on the increase, comes to 2,370 diocesan and 1,600 religious.

In an address on January 18, 1939, Pius XI had already referred to the missionary vocation of the Philippines. This theme was taken up again in Paul VI's address to the Philippine bishops on November 29, 1970, before he left Manila:

> At this moment one cannot help thinking of the important vocation of the Filipino people. This country is called in a very special way to be the city on the mountain, the lamp on the pedestal (Matt. 5:14–16), and to be a radiant witness in the midst of the ancient and noble Asian cultures.

John Paul II confirmed this missionary vocation even more explicitly. In his address to the Filipino episcopate in Manila on February 17, 1981, he stated that the church of the Philippines undoubtedly has a special missionary vocation despite its limited resources:

> Paul VI confirmed this missionary vocation of yours during his visit here and repeatedly thereafter. From many points of

view, dear brothers, you are truly called to be a missionary church.

He came back to this point during his visit to Baguio on February 22. Having paid homage to the church of the Philippines for its vitality, he then referred to *ad extra* missionary expansion:

> I wish to tell you of my special desire, that the Filipinos will become the principal missionaries of the church in Asia. . . . Has not the Lord of history destined you to play a prominent role in the missionary effort of the church in this region ? . . . This is my heartfelt desire and my fervent prayer: that you may now take your place in the forefront of the church's missionary effort, especially here in Asia.

Later, in Rome, he returned to this point during an audience on March 3, 1981. In his address he praised the Philippine bishops for their initiative in founding a missionary institute and pointed out the very important missionary work performed by Radio Veritas, whose broadcasts in twelve languages reach many countries in East, Central, and South Asia.

Missionary Institutes

At the suggestion of the bishop of Dumaguete, the Philippine episcopal conference decided in 1965 to open the Missionary Society of the Philippines, an institute for diocesan priests. In 1978 the institute had 12 priests and 19 major seminarians. Six of these priests are working in other Asian countries. Lack of greater success is probably due to the fact that, remaining an episcopal initiative, it has not become an autonomous agency.

It is especially through the channel of the international religious institutes that the Philippines is becoming an evangelizing nation. These institutes, which have large numbers of indigenous members, are sending Filipino missionaries all over the world.

In 1972 about 400 Filipino missionaries were working abroad. Ten years later their number (priests, brothers, sisters, and lay persons) had doubled. Among them are 115 priests. The institutes for men that are sending out a sizable number of missionaries (priests and brothers) are the S.V.D. Fathers, 58; the C.I.C.M. Fathers, 33; the Jesuits, 21; the Oblates, 19; and the Salesians, 15. In 1981 the bishop of Sorsogon decided to send out priests to the U.S.A. to work among Filipinos residing there. Philippine missionaries are working in 60 dioceses outside the Philippines. A preparatory course for missionaries who will serve *ad extra* was launched in Tagaytay (diocese of Imus).

Among the 800 missionaries, there are 410 sisters: Franciscan Missionaries of Mary, 54; Daughters of Charity, 45; I.C.M. Sisters (Heverlee), 40; Sisters of the Good Shepherd, 33; Maryknoll Sisters, 30; Sisters of St. Paul de Chartres, 30.

The Philippine Lay Mission Volunteers, an association of lay missionaries, was founded in 1976. Three mission teams have been sent to Africa and Latin America. They are working in ten different places in the Philippines. The Maryknoll Fathers give their assistance to this association.

Thanks to the international character of these sending institutes, Filipino missionaries are already spread all over the world. Filipino C.I.C.M. Fathers are working in Zambia, Nigeria (where one was murdered), Taiwan, Indonesia, Japan, the Dominican Republic, Brazil, Mexico, and Guatemala (where one was murdered by government accomplices). Filipino S.V.D. missionaries are working in Indonesia, Taiwan, Ghana, New Guinea, Argentina, Brazil, and Paraguay. Filipina I.C.M. sisters are working in Hong Kong, Taiwan, India, Burundi, Zaire, Cameroon, Haiti, the Caribbean, Guatemala, Brazil, the U.S.A., and Europe. In 1982, 4 Filipino Jesuits left for mission work in Korea. A Filipina Daughter of Charity has been sent to Korea, where she is to pursue missionary work with five Indian Daughters of Charity.

This shows how mission of today and tomorrow is acquiring an international and supranational character.

"Local Church" Means "Sending Church"

A major event for Asia and especially for the Philippines with regard to evangelization was the well-organized International Congress on Mission held in Manila, December 2 to 7, 1979. It dealt with the theme "The Good News of God's Kingdom to the Peoples of Asia." The initiative came from Bishop G. Rosales, at that time auxiliary bishop of Manila and national director of the Pontifical Mission Aid Societies.

Among the 200 participants there were 89 official delegates from 35 Asian countries. Their reflection on evangelization of the Asian countries was very thorough. An analysis of the Asian context served as the starting point to determine the priorities of an evangelization adapted to the de facto situation on the continent. They stressed that today the Asian churches themselves are responsible for the evangelization of Asia, but at the same time they expressed their concern for the evangelization of the world. Foreign missionaries are always welcome "not only as living signs of the universality of the church, but also because, having different Christian and cultural backgrounds, they can enrich and challenge the local church."

The congress proved that the church of Asia has come to a turning point in its history and that a new mission period has begun. Thus we read in the final message of the congress:

> What is the newness of this "new age of mission?" First, the realization in practice that "mission" is no longer, and can no longer be, a one-way movement from the "older churches" to the "younger churches," from the churches of the old christendom to the churches in the colonial lands. Now—as Vatican II already affirmed with all clarity and force—every local church is and cannot but be missionary. Every local church is "sent" by Christ and the Father to bring the gospel to its surrounding milieu, and to bear it also to all the world. For every local church this is a primary task. Hence we are moving beyond the vocabulary and the idea of "sending churches" and "receiving churches," for, as living communities of the one church of Jesus Christ, every local church must be a sending church, and every local church (because it is not ever on earth a total realization of the church) must also be a receiving church. Every local church is responsible for its mission, and co-responsible for the mission of all its sister churches. Every local church, according to its possibilities, must share whatever its gifts are, for the needs of other

churches, for mission throughout mankind, for the life of the world. . . .

We have reached a decisive turning point in the mission history of the Third World. There is no return to the past, neither to past mission theories, nor to past mission methods, nor to past mission goals.

With regard to the Philippines, the chairman of the congress, Bishop Rosales, said for his part:

> The Christian faith was planted in our land some four hundred and sixty years ago; the "mustard seed" has become a tree with a multitude of branches and leaves. . . . Our church, though [it] still has weaknesses, has become powerful; the task of evangelization challenges [it].

At the July 1980 meeting of the episcopal conference, the bishop stated:

> Although our present shortage of priests is one of the sharpest of the world, our people must become missionary; we must send missionaries and support them financially. Because of their rich apostolic potential the Philippines are called upon to evangelize Asia. The Philippine missionaries are very well suited for this work, because they understand the Eastern mentality and are able to go and work without any colonial ties, because coming from a poor country they can understand people in poor countries and adapt to their way of life.

India

India is called upon to play an important part in future world events. As of 1980, it had many more inhabitants (683.8 million), than Africa (469.5 million), more than the whole of North America (616.8 million), and almost double that of Latin America (365 million). India houses 15 percent of the world population. By the end of this century, one human being out of six will be from India. The peoples of India are dynamic, endowed with rich cultures and renowned religions. However

India is also a country of widespread poverty and of terrifying social injustices.

In this vast country there is a lively church. It has an impressive apostolic potential, not only with regard to quantity, but also with regard to quality. No other Asian church has so many scholars, theologians, faculties of theology, pastoral institutes, theological and pastoral reviews. The Indian church can make use of the cultural and religious wealth of the peoples of India as an instrument for further reflection on the good news and for better understanding its own mission. Except for the church of Vietnam, no other young church depends so much on its own resources as does India. More than any other young church it can share with others the wealth of its own personnel and spiritual values. In the years to come, it will be called upon to be one of the pillars of the universal church.

Church Statistics

According to the latest statistics available (1980), India counts 11.3 million Catholics out of a total population of 684 million— 1.7 percent. In terms of world *Christian* population, India accounts for 2.6 percent. Even though this percentage is quite small, Christianity ranks third among Indian religions, after Hinduism (82 percent) and Islam (12 percent), but ahead of Sikhism (2 percent) and Buddhism (0.7 percent). 81 percent of the Catholics reside in southern and western India. Northern India is still an immense mission territory.

- There are 110 Indian dioceses. Of the 126 bishops, only 3 are non-Indian. Most of the 41 religious bishops reside in northern India, where evangelization has hardly begun.
- Of the 11,733 priests, there are 6,828 diocesan and 4,905 religious (41 percent). Only 841 priests are expatriate. Religious priests are members of 39 different institutes, 11 of which were founded in India; 8 of them belong to Eastern rites.
- More than 1,300 of the 2,994 brothers belong to congregations of brothers only, 11 of which are of Indian origin. Among the brothers there are only 136 non-Indian.
- The 50,936 religious women belong to 166 congregations, 64

of which were founded in India. There are but 1,213 foreign religious sisters.
- Of the 4,995 major seminarians, 2,916 are diocesan and 2,079 religious. After the U.S.A., Italy, and Poland, India has the largest number of seminarians in the world. There are 30 major seminaries (diocesan and religious), 7 of which are theological institutes.
- With some 300 members in all, 14 secular institutes are pursuing their apostolate in India; 6 of them are of Indian origin.

Kerala

Within the national church of India, the regional church of Kerala deserves special mention. About 4 million Catholics—a third of the Indian church—live in the state of Kerala. Among them, Catholics of Eastern rites—Syro-Malabar and Syro-Malankar—constitute the majority (2.7 million). They are the descendants of the St. Thomas Christians. Among them the Syro-Malankars (united to Rome in 1930) form a minority. Eastern-rite Catholics constitute 25 percent of all Indian Catholics and have 34 percent of the priests. Their 10 indigenous congregations for men (2,218 members) count 35 percent of all religious men in India. The 23 indigenous congregations for women (18,977 members) count 40 percent of all religious women in India. Kerala also has 5,000 religious men and women of the Latin rite. If we add the numbers of priests and sisters of the Latin rite to those of the Eastern rites, we find that 50 percent of the priests and 60 percent of the religious come from Kerala. Kerala has one vocation (priest, brother, sister) for every 70 Catholics (in the diocese of Palai, 1 for every 32 Catholics). The Syro-Malabars have two major seminaries, one at Alwaye with 453 seminarians and one at Kottayam with 324 seminarians. In addition, the Carmelites of Mary Immaculate have a theological training center in Bangalore.

The church of Kerala is not only a church very rich in vocations, it is also a redoubtable missionary church. In fact, it has more priests, brothers, and sisters than it needs for its own purposes; 45 percent of its priests and 65 percent of its sisters migrate to other regions of India. Consequently, the Syro-Malabars are spread all over the subcontinent. Adhering to their own rites, they create problems when working in dioceses of the Latin rite. Territories of northern India have been entrusted to them. Seven dioceses in Chanda and in the north have become Eastern-rite dioceses. Five of them were entrusted to the Carmelites of Mary Immaculate, one to the Missionary Society of St. Thomas the Apostle, and one to the Vincentian Congregation. These dioceses have but few Catholics; they are genuine mission territories.

That Syro-Malabar priests and sisters are being sent out *ad extra* does not necessarily mean that they are always animated by a true missionary spirit—that is, that they are pursuing the direct evangelization of non-Christians according to the new missionary methods (inculturation, interreligious dialogue, commitment to development and liberation). As a matter of fact this caveat does not apply only to priests from Kerala. Many Indian priests are still adhering to their traditional methods or are satisfied with establishing Christian ghettos. In India, and especially in the south, much remains to be done among priests and religious to animate them with a true missionary spirit for evangelization *ad intra*, and even more so for evangelization *ad extra*.

The Little Flower Mission League (with 300,000 members in 1968) was founded in 1947 in Kerala to promote a missionary spirit. The Missionary Society of St. Thomas the Apostle (Palai) was established in 1968. In 1977 it had 30 priests, 81 minor seminarians, and 100 major seminarians. The diocese of Ujjain was entrusted to this society.

The Carmelites of Mary Immaculate, founded in 1855, is a flourishing Syro-Malabar congregation for religious men. It has 1,415 members, including 886 priests. As mentioned before, five mission dioceses have been entrusted to this congregation. Other congregations of men are the Vincentian Congregation, founded in 1927 (244 members, including 114 priests), the Little Flower Congregation, founded in 1947 (80 priests, 30 brothers, 68 scholastics, 20 novices).

A Deepening Missionary Spirit

At the 1969 All India Seminar it was agreed upon that a missionary spirit ought to be fostered among priests, that a course in missiology should be incorporated into all seminary curricula, that a textbook had to be compiled on methods of evangelization in India, that more Indian sisters ought to be trained for direct evangelization, that the church of India should become more self-reliant. It was also agreed upon that the southern dioceses with copious priests should supply personnel to the mission dioceses of the north.

It is common knowledge that the southern dioceses, with large numbers of Catholics and of priests, are more conservative and less mission-minded. The missionary spirit is very much alive in the north—for example, in the Ranchi district, which, after Kerala, is becoming a new dynamic pole of the Indian church.

In 1974 the 13 bishops of Tamil Nadu decided to open an interdiocesan seminary to train priests who would work in northern India. This seminary, Xavier Mission House, was opened in the diocese of Kottar. In 1981 it had 86 students. At the FABC meeting in Taipei, an Indian bishop said that it was almost as difficult for a priest from the south to adjust to living in the north as it would be for a foreign missionary.

Some dioceses have begun to send Fidei Donum priests to other continents. The archdiocese of Goa has a team of diocesan priests working in Venezuela. The archdiocese of Bombay is also sending priests to Latin America.

India has had its own missionary institutes for some years. But it is only of late that they have started to flourish. We have already dealt with the Syro-Malabar congregations. Two mission institutes (of Latin rite) were founded in northern India. The Society of the Missionaries of St. Francis Xavier, also known as the Society of Pilar, was founded in 1887 in Goa. After its reorganization in 1939, it became an authentically missionary institute. Its members are working among the non-Christians of India. In 1977 the institute had 105 priests, 27 brothers, 48 scholastics, and 7 novices. The Indian Missionary Society, founded in 1943 at Varanasi (Benares) by Father Gaspar Pinto, is another missionary institute. It is performing missionary work in nine dioceses of India and in the Fiji Islands. The institute recently went through a crisis, but in 1980 it had 48 priests, 22 brothers, 69 scholastics, and 15 novices.

Various recent initiatives show how fast the missionary spirit is growing all over India. The country has quite a number of valuable theological reviews at its disposal—for example, *Indian Theological Studies* (Bangalore), *Vidyajyoti* (Delhi), *Jeevadhara* (Kottayam, Kerala), *Word and Worship* (Bangalore). Quite a number of articles in these reviews deal with problems of evangelization in India. The famous National, Biblical, Catechetical, and Liturgical Center of Bangalore, for many years directed by the respected theologian D.S. Amalorpavadass, plays an important part in Indian theological reflection and pastoral renewal. India has a growing number of renowned theologians, whose contributions to theological and missiological reflection are appreciated even outside India.

In September 1976 the S.V.D. Fathers opened a center for missiological studies and formation at Ishvan Kendra (diocese of Poona). In 1977 the Missionary Society of St. Thomas the Apostle opened a training institute at Kamed to prepare Syro-Malabar missionaries for evangelization among Hindus and Muslims. In 1979 the Salesian Fathers started issuing a valuable missiological journal, *Indian Missiological Review* (Shillong).

In 1980 the St. Peter Pontifical Seminary of Bangalore started offering a two-year course in missiology. The first of its kind in India, the course presents mission studies, with special reference to India, to students who will later plan, coordinate, and effectively carry out missionary activities at all levels. Almost all seminaries, as well as pastoral centers, have missiological courses on their programs.

Religious Institutes

The impulse for mission *ad extra* is fostered mainly by the international religious institutes that have branches in India. Their Indian provinces have many Indian members. Some institutes are divided into more than one province and have many vocations. As mentioned before, the Jesuits have about 3,000 local members, spread over 11 provinces and vice-provinces (77 percent of their members are from India and Sri Lanka). In 1980 the Salesians (4 provinces) counted 1,350 professed members and 121 novices. In 1981 the S.V.D. Fathers had 267 professed members, of whom 224 were Indian (181 priests).

India has a total of 166 congregations for religious women. In general, the indigenous congregations count many members. Some of them have sisters working in Europe or in North America. Some years ago, the world press spread the news about a certain "trade in girls"—an initiative of some priests (from Kerala), who provided candidates or alleged candidates for religious congregations of women in the West anxious to fill their empty novitiates. This sensational news, having some foundation, resulted in the suppression of this unhealthy practice.

Quite a number of religious sisters are involved in pastoral and social activities. Many of them follow courses at universities or at pastoral and theological centers. Several centers for pastoral training have been created expressly for religious sisters.

As mentioned above, the number of religious women is highest in Kerala. The Congregation of the Mother of Carmel, founded in 1866 and reorganized in 1969 through the fusion of several congregations, had 3,961 professed members and 91 novices in 1977.

Most international congregations of religious women have large numbers of Indian members. The Franciscan Missionaries of Mary (founded in India) have 1,226 Indian members and 21 novices in their five provinces. The Sisters of St. Anne, founded in 1909 in Lucerne, have 455 members and 77 candidates in India, whereas in Switzerland they have but 286 members and 2 candidates (1981). The Daughters of the Holy Cross (Liège, Belgium) have 324 professed members (almost all indigenous) and 16 novices. The Ursulines of Tildonck (Belgium) have 380 professed members and 23 novices. The I.C.M. Sisters (Heverlee) have 175 Indian members and 23 novices. The Sisters of Charity (Ghent, Belgium) have 220 professed members (most of them Indian) and 22 novices.

Evangelization ad extra

A sign of India's missionary maturity and a symbol of its worldwide influence are the foundations of Mother Teresa: the Missionary Sisters of Charity (founded in 1950) and the Missionary Brothers of Charity (founded in 1963). These foundations and their astounding expansion are indeed a marvel. In 1980 they had 1,800 sisters, 500 brothers, 354 novices (men and women), and 150 houses. Besides John Paul II, there is probably nobody else in the church whose witness is so evangelizing as Mother Teresa's. The question can be raised whether there was any other country in the world so well suited to allow the wonder of Mother Teresa and her foundations to come about.

Mission *ad extra* has definitely been launched in India. At present, Indian missionaries sent *ad extra* outnumber the foreign missionaries working in India. According to estimates, more than 2,000 Indian missionaries are working abroad. India is giving more than it is receiving.

Indian missionaries, men and women, are working in other Asian countries and in many countries of the other continents. Indian Jesuits are working in Pakistan, Nepal, Bhutan, the Fiji Islands, British Guyana, Mauritius, Kenya, Tanzania, Sudan, Zaire. There are 30 Jesuits working in Nepal and another 30 in East Africa. Fifteen Indian Salesians left for Africa in 1980 (Kenya, Tanzania, Sudan). Indian I.C.M. Sisters are working in Brazil, the Caribbean, and Europe. Twenty Mission Sisters of the Queen of Apostles (Bombay) have gone to Australia.

India has become the most important missionary country of the third church. And this is but a beginning. We can foresee that in the future India will be one of the most important evangelizing countries. The apostolic potential of the Indian Catholic Church is more important than that of any other Third World church. It can avail itself of the dynamism and the spiritual wealth of the Indian people.

At present, bishops in need of personnel, especially the bishops of Africa, are appealing to Polish bishops and institutes. Poland has been undergoing an ever increasing missionary expansion. It sends out about one hundred new missionaries every year. It is the only Western country with such a potential. However, Poland cannot satisfy all the demands. Has the time not come for bishops to turn to India for missionaries?

Korea

The foundation of the church in Korea (1784) is something unique in church history. It was founded by Korean lay persons who, having come to know Christianity on the occasion of a visit to Peking, spread it clandestinely in their own country. The church of Korea is a church of martyrs. It has often known persecution, especially during the nineteenth century. In 1984 the church solemnly celebrates its bi-centennial.

Relying almost exclusively on its own resources, the Korean church in recent years has become a flourishing and dynamic church. But it has been facing a situation of conflict because of its option in defense of human rights.

Some statistics, as of the end of 1980:

- 1.3 million Catholics (3.3 percent of the total population, the highest percentage in Asia after the Philippines, Vietnam, and Sri Lanka). There are 35,000 catechumens and 10,000 persons taking correspondence catechism courses;
- 19 bishops (of whom 4 are non-Korean);
- 1,107 priests (797 diocesan and 310 religious), of whom only 259 are expatriate;
- 201 brothers, of whom 45 are expatriate;
- 3,165 sisters, of whom 169 are expatriate;
- 658 major seminarians: 569 diocesan and 89 religious.

There are many vocations to the priesthood. Two of the three major seminaries are overcrowded (as of 1982): Seoul (333 students), Kwang-ju (370). There are no minor seminaries. Many seminarians have university degrees and have completed three years of military service.

Over the last two decades there has been an increase of half a million Catholics. The numerical growth of Catholics (6 percent) exceeds the population growth (1.8 percent). The numerical increase of Protestants has been spectacular: 4 million since 1974. All told, there are about 6.5 million Christians. Next to the Philippines, Korea has become the most Christian country of Asia.

If this amazing movement of conversion persists, half of South Korea might be Christian by the end of the century. A recent baptism celebration could have happened only in Korea: among fourteen adults baptized, there were five former ministers of state, three members of Parliament, and a former Air Force chief of staff. Their catechist was the former minister-president Dr. Chang, himself a convert.

Because of persecution and foreign occupation, the church of Korea remained for a long time a self-confined church. But now it has become conscious of its potentialities. It dedicates itself to intense *ad intra* evangelization and has begun to be concerned about *ad extra* evangelization.

In 1975 Bishop J. Choi took the initiative of founding a missionary institute, the Korean Missionary Society. He said, "For two hundred years we have been receiving help from the universal church. Now the time has come to give." Within a few years he had the backing of the bishops' conference. In 1978 the administration of the institute was entrusted to Bishop Kim Nal Su (Su-Won). The institute counted 8 priests and 23 seminarians in 1981. In November 1981 the first four missionaries were sent out, to New Guinea. An association has also been founded to support the missionary institute and missionary work financially. It counts five hundred members. Foreign mission must become the concern of the whole Korean church.

The bishops decided to prepare their faithful over a period of four years for a solemn 1984 bicentennial celebration. In their March 1981 pastoral letter, they summoned the faithful to organize a decisive missionary activity. For each year they proposed a theme to be reflected upon. "Evangelization of the neighbor" was the theme for 1981. All the baptized were urged to proclaim the gospel in their own surroundings. That same year there were 118,485 baptisms, including 87,350 adult baptisms. The bishops' promptings launched a real movement of conversion. In 1984 the whole Korean church is in a state of mission.

Japan

Japan witnessed a flourishing Christianity during the sixteenth and seventeenth centuries. It could easily have become a Christian country. But several unfortunate circumstances led to persecutions, which systematically rooted out Christianity. The church might have survived, if it had had sufficient resources of its own. It was only a century ago that mission work could be resumed. The flourishing period which the church experienced at the end of World War II has since come to a certain stagnation.

At the end of 1980 there were but 398,000 Catholics out of 117 million inhabitants (at the end of 1981: 411,451)—less than 1 percent. All told, there are about 1.1 million Christians. But Christianity exerts a great influence. Official surveys reveal that more than 3 million Japanese declare themselves to be Christian. Even though there is a great interest in Christianity, few are those who join the official churches.

In proportion to the number of Catholics, Japan has very many priests (1 for every 198 Catholics) and sisters (1 for every 54 Catholics), but there is only one priest for every 59,000 Japanese. Consequently, foreign help remains badly needed.

Some statistics, as of the end of 1981:

- 16 residential bishops (all of them Japanese);
- 884 indigenous priests (508 diocesan and 376 religious); foreign priests number 1,013;
- 5,988 indigenous sisters, 692 expatriate (in Japan there is one sister for every 33 Catholic women!);
- 216 indigenous brothers; 142 non-Japanese;
- 179 major seminarians: 84 diocesan and 95 religious.

The growth in vocations has since come to a standstill.

The concern for *ad extra* mission is not very much alive yet in Japan. If the number of priests and sisters is very high in proportion to the number of Catholics, it is very small in proportion to the millions of non-Christians. It is understandable that little attention is paid to the sending of missionaries to other countries.

The Japanese bishops are challenged by the missionary impulse launched by the 1974 synod of bishops, by *Evangelii Nuntiandi*, and by the FABC. In May 1977 they studied a plan to found a Japanese society for foreign mission. Bishops and priests met in October 1979 to discuss the theme of missionary evangelization in Japan.

According to 1982 records, 215 Japanese missionaries are working abroad: 58 elsewhere in Asia, 110 in Latin America, 20 in Africa and the Near East, 27 in Europe. They are working especially among Japanese living abroad, particularly in Brazil (69 missionaries). The Sisters of the Immaculate Heart of Mary

(Nagasaki) have sent out six sisters to the Amazon region. There are more Japanese Catholics in Brazil (about 900,000) than in Japan, but many of those in Brazil are only superficially Catholic. In Asia, Japanese missionaries are present in regions almost inaccessible to Christian mission—for example, Japanese Sisters of Notre Dame (Namur) and Japanese Jesuits are serving in Nepal. The Franciscan Missionaries of Mary have 364 Japanese members; 43 of them are working abroad (11 in 8 African countries, 6 in 4 Asian countries, and 9 in Brazil). Japanese missionaries have not been sent by their bishops; they have been sent by their religious institutes or they have set out on their own initiative.

Vietnam

The church of Vietnam has a glorious past. In the course of its history it continually faced trials and often bloody persecutions. In this respect it can be compared to the church of the first centuries. In the second half of the nineteenth century alone, 115 Vietnamese priests, hundreds of sisters and catechists, and a hundred thousand Christians were murdered. The church has not only survived these persecutions, but has been strengthened by them. This is mainly because, more than any other local church, it had a large number of indigenous priests, sisters, and catechists. Even today this church is continually facing trials. In spite of them, Vietnam has become, next to the Philippines and Sri Lanka, the most Catholic country of Asia (Sri Lanka's percentage of Catholics is slightly higher). No other Third World church has so many resources of its own.

After the Geneva treaty of July 21, 1954, which divided Vietnam in two, many Catholics (600,000) and many priests migrated to the south. Hence it is also in the south that the church enjoys the greatest vitality (10 percent of the population is Catholic). Since the northern invasion and the surrender of Saigon on April 20, 1975—in other words, since the unification and the independence of the nation—the church has relied exclusively on its own resources. Today it faces fierce oppression once more. From the scant information available, it seems that it will be able to resist. We can surely hope that, like the church of

Poland, it will not only be able to survive, but gain in strength and depth under a communist regime. Vietnam can be considered the "Asian Poland."

The continuous hardships and wars have isolated the church of Vietnam and prevented it from training its own scholars and theologians. Its influence *ad extra* has been minimal. Yet missionary consciousness had awakened a long time ago. Indeed the Vietnamese church had become very dynamic and had many resources at its disposal.

Fr. Dominique Marie Tran Dinh Thy founded a missionary institute, the Congregation of the Mother Co-Redemptrix, in 1953 in the diocese of Buichu (North Vietnam). It envisaged mission in Vietnam and elsewhere in Asia. The congregation has suffered severe trials: the communist capture of Hanoi (1954), the flight to South Vietnam, the 1975 invasion by the Vietcong. In 1975 the congregation counted 11 priests, 110 seminarians, 30 novices. Before the invasion by the north, 166 members had migrated to the U.S.A.

In 1970 the bishops set up their National Commission for Evangelization. In addition, each bishop was asked to set up a similar diocesan committee, as well as parochial mission boards. Every bishop was invited to create a diocesan fund to support the missionary work of the Pontifical Mission Aid Societies.

In 1973 the bishops decided to found the Vietnamese Missionary Society. Its supervision was entrusted to Archbishop Nguyen Kim Dien (Hué), a Little Brother of Charles de Foucauld. The Foreign Missions of Paris took care of its technical aspects. The society had a good start. In 1975 it counted 6 priests and 6 seminarians. We do not know how this initiative has fared since then.

Some statistics for Vietnam (North and South combined):

- 3.5 million Catholics out of a total population of 52.7 million (6.6 percent);
- 25 dioceses;
- 2,200 priests;
- 1,000 major seminarians;
- 6,520 sisters.

More recent, unofficial statistics (1981) mention 43 bishops, 2,500 priests, 7,000 sisters.

Like the church of Poland, the church of Vietnam lives in a situation of conflict. In Poland this situation resulted in a purification and a renewed dynamism, which paved the way for a missionary breakthrough. Perhaps history will repeat itself in Vietnam.

Sri Lanka

The church of Sri Lanka has a fascinating history, quite similar to that of the church of India, its neighbor. Because of the high percentage of Catholics (6.8 percent), its influence on public life is more influential than that of the church in India. Next to the Philippines and together with Vietnam, Sri Lanka has the highest percentage of Catholics in Asian countries.

Some statistics, as of 1981:

- 14.9 million inhabitants;
- 1,009,577 Catholics (6.8 percent). The number of Protestants is estimated at about 300,000. Hence the percentage of all Christians amounts to 8.8 percent;
- 9 dioceses (all 13 bishops are Sri Lankan);
- 570 priests: 346 diocesan and 224 religious (more than 90 percent of the priests are Sri Lankan; their number is increasing, but very slowly; in 1974 there were 338 diocesan priests);
- 220 major seminarians: 193 diocesan and 27 religious (a total of 192 in 1974);
- 325 brothers;
- 2,375 sisters: more than 90 percent are Sri Lankan.

The church of Sri Lanka, formerly fairly well structured, with many institutions at its disposal and quite occidental, clerical, and turned in upon itself, has been hard hit in recent decades. In 1960 the schools were nationalized. In 1971 the church encountered strong opposition from the new leftist government and from Marxist and ultranationalist circles, especially among Sri Lankan youth. This compelled it to intensify the self-criticism initiated by Vatican II. The church has changed. Aggiornamento coincided with a severe inner crisis, which has not yet been completely overcome. The church integrates itself more and more in the culture of the people and collaborates closely with the other religions: Buddhism (69 percent of the national population), Hinduism (15.5 percent), and Islam (7.6 percent). It defends the rights of the poor and of minorities. It, or at least its more progressive wing, is socially committed. The renowned Center for Religion and Society, founded at Colombo in 1970, plays an important part in this evolution. In a country with at times heavy racial and social tensions, the church has an important mission to fulfill.

Due to several causes, the number of conversions has declined, notwithstanding the church's inner renewal and great influence.

Statistics reveal that the church of Sri Lanka has a very high percentage of indigenous personnel. From this point of view it is a strong church. It is also the church of a dynamic people. Thus it is easy to understand that a missionary movement has been developing for quite some time—namely, since 1968. Missionary institutes in Sri Lanka started sending out their Sri Lankan members. Sri Lanka has become a missionary country, even though there is but one priest for every 1,771 Catholics and for every 26,000 inhabitants.

In 1982 there were 110 missionaries working in other Asian countries (Pakistan, India, Bangladesh, Malaysia, and Korea), in Africa, and in Latin America. Pakistan alone has 18 priests, 21 brothers, and 36 sisters from Sri Lanka.

CHAPTER FOUR

THE RISE OF MISSIONARY CONSCIOUSNESS IN LATIN AMERICA

The church of Latin America, stagnating in the nineteenth century, recovered at the beginning of the present century thanks to outside aid. From the time of Vatican II onward, it has been regaining its vitality. John XXIII pointed to the emergency situation of the Latin American church and addressed an urgent appeal to the churches of Europe and North America, asking their help before it would be too late. God's Spirit has been very active in the Latin American church. It is very surprising to see how it has, in a very short time, become a young, dynamic, and prophetic church.

The Latin American countries form a huge Catholic bloc; in years to come, it will count half of all Catholics in the world. In these countries, religion and culture are closely interwoven. Ecclesial renewal is borne by the deep religiosity of the Latin American peoples.

The Latin American church is the first church to reverse a mistake that all other churches have been guilty of in previous centuries. It dissociated itself from its powerful and rich allies and turned to the masses of the poor, the emarginated, the oppressed. By choosing to be "for, with, and equal to" the poor, it has become a leading model for church renewal. In fidelity to the gospel, the example of this church suggests an examination of conscience appropriate to other churches. The Latin American church is also struggling to free itself from the aftermath of colonialism that still affects the African and Asian churches.

As a consequence of its prophetic action, the church of Latin America is being oppressed and persecuted. Thus it shares in the sufferings of Christ and becomes more and more assimilated to the Redeemer. Christ's words, that the gospel would be a stumbling block and a sign of contradiction, are being verified in it.

Other churches realize more and more that it is in Latin America that models for church renewal must be looked for. The major contemporary trends in renewed pastoral reflection have come from Latin America: church upbuilding from the grass roots, liberation theology, and re-evaluation of popular religiosity. By identifying itself with the poor, the Latin American church has become a church of hope, spiritually rich, young, and full of life.

Missionary Commitment *ad extra*

Vatican II has been a blessing for the Latin American church. So also was the CELAM general meeting in Medellín in September 1968; in line with the council, it drafted a program for Latin American church renewal. It was a major event for Latin America. The CELAM meeting in Puebla, Mexico (Jan. 27 to Feb. 13, 1979), under the theme "Evangelization in Latin America's Present and Future," became an important event for the whole church. Henceforth, all churches are watching what is being done in Latin America.

Latin American church renewal has been heavily influenced by CELAM. Founded in 1955, it has served as a model for the creation of the continental bishops' conferences of Africa, Europe, and Asia.

It is not my purpose to point out all the aspects of Latin American church renewal, with its successes and problems. I wish here to point out only that one crucial church problem—the shortage of priests—is gradually being solved. For the past few years, records of the number of priests reveal a steady growth. This proves that the Latin American church is recovering its strength.

In the course of five years (1975 to 1980), the number of Latin American major seminarians increased from 636 to 1,373 in

Argentina; from 2,667 to 4,283 in Brazil; from 442 to 663 in Chile; from 1,259 to 1,857 in Colombia; from 402 to 693 in Peru; from 206 to 371 in Venezuela; from 129 to 286 in the Dominican Republic; from 87 to 139 in Haiti. There was not one major seminarian in Santiago (Chile) in 1971; in 1981 there were 121. In Córdoba (Argentina) there were 12 seminarians in 1970, but 150 in 1981. From 1964 to 1970 São Paulo (Brazil) had but two priestly ordinations; but there were 64 new priests for the years 1980 and 1981. This is but the beginning of a revival. In some other countries, however, the numbers have not increased.

It is well to note that growth is observed especially in those countries where the church goes to the people, where its work is done more and more by the basic communities. The people of God, the base, provides priestly and religious vocations. Pope John Paul II stated on July 2, 1980, in Rio de Janeiro:

> Priestly vocations ought to be the sign of the maturity of communities, the result of entrusting ministries to lay persons, the consequence of sound schooling and family pastoral ministry.

Since the time of Medellín the theme of evangelization has frequently been discussed in Latin America. It should not surprise us that until recently it was almost exclusively restricted to *ad intra* evangelization. The needs *ad intra* are so great that nobody thought about supplying personnel for *ad extra* evangelization.

Today things have changed in this respect. The Latin American church has understood that it too has a part to play in world evangelization.

The mission department of CELAM, with its manifold national ramifications, is playing an important part in stimulating this new consciousness. The national episcopal commissions for mission are more and more concerned about the problem of *ad extra* evangelization. In this respect, as in so many others, the Episcopal Conference of Brazil, with its 230 dioceses, is taking the lead.

Thanks to CELAM, Latin America is the only continent where there is such close and well-organized cooperation among the national episcopal conferences. Thanks to the Latin American Conference of Religious (CLAR), no other continent enjoys such close cooperation among religious institutes. Moreover, there is excellent collaboration between CELAM and the CLAR. This is of paramount importance, inasmuch as the majority of priests in Latin America are religious (25,497 religious and 23,281 diocesan priests). In Latin America there is a fine spirit of mutual collaboration, joint reflection and action. Cooperation between churches is much easier in Latin America than in any other continent because their situations and problems are basically the same. Besides, for the most part only two languages—and cognate languages at that—are spoken.

This spirit of cooperation is manifested in the promotion of a missionary spirit (*ad extra* mission). The mission department of CELAM works in close cooperation with the national directors of the Pontifical Mission Aid Societies and the religious institutes. Many initiatives are taken jointly. In Latin America the national directors of the Pontifical Mission Aid Societies show that they have grasped that their first task consists in stimulating the missionary consciousness of the entire people of God.

Several countries organize regular national mission congresses, which know an ever growing success. The seventh national mission congress of Mexico took place in November 1977 at Torreón. Its closing session was attended by 20,000 lay persons, 3,000 sisters, 1,000 priests, and 100 bishops. Colombia had its third national mission congress in October 1982. Ecuador had a national mission congress in March 1982, attended by about 7,000 young persons. The 1981 and 1982 national mission congresses aimed at preparing for the continental Latin American mission congress in Mexico in 1983. The national mission congresses of Argentina (1981), Bolivia (1981), and Peru (1982) had the same objective.

As for other pastoral activities, so also for missionary activity, there was a felt need for reflection and cooperation on the continental level. The mission department of CELAM, the Pontifical Mission Aid Societies, and the missionary institutes took the initiative of organizing the first international meeting for missionary reflection and planning at Tlaxcala (Mexico) in August 1980. They wanted to pursue the Puebla reflection on mission. They insisted on giving a new impulse to missionary animation, on adding a missionary dimension to catechesis, especially to catechesis of the young, and on instilling a missionary openness in the basic ecclesial communities. They decided to create COMLA (Congreso Misionero Latinoamericano). During the meeting, Bishop L. Munive Escobar, bishop of Tlaxcala and president of the CELAM mission department, stated:

> Perhaps we are too busy with our poverty, our needs, and our problems. We are too much convinced that we must first possess in order to give, and that the church of Latin America is not yet in a position to give. Here I do not refer to money, but to missionaries, to aid and services in their various forms. We should reply that "giving" is not a question of "having" but of "being." If we are truly church, we must give from our poverty. We must go beyond our borders. We suppose that our missionary commitment *ad extra* ought to be the fruit of evangelization in Latin America. The contrary is true. Missionary commitment *ad extra* will be proof of the authenticity and validity of Latin American evangelization *ad intra*.

Just as the delegates of the bishops' conferences regularly meet for CELAM and the representatives of the religious institutes for CLAR gatherings, so also those responsible for mission come together periodically for Latin American mission congresses.

In Tlaxcala, it was decided that a second Latin American mission congress (COMLA II) would be held from May 17 to May 21, 1983. The congress was prepared for very carefully. Its aim was to awaken a missionary spirit in Latin American local churches.

In recent years, four centers have been created for missionary training: in Mexico, near the shrine of Our Lady of Guadalupe; in Brasilia (Brazil); in Buenos Aires, for Spanish-speaking South America. And an international center for the training of diocesan priests for mission *ad extra* was opened in Lima in 1981.

Mexico

It is evident that Mexico plays an important role in the growing missionary movement in Latin America. For more than thirty years, Mexico has had its own missionary institute, the

Institute of Our Lady of Guadalupe for Foreign Missions. Founded in 1949, it could rely on the technical assistance of the Maryknoll missionaries. It has long had the bishops' full support. As of 1982, it numbers 102 priests and 110 candidates to the priesthood. It has sent missionaries to Japan, Korea, Kenya, Hong Kong, and Angola. In 1977 the archbishop of Luanda (Angola) asked it to take charge of his major seminary. Twenty members of the institute are working in Korea. Some seminarians are being trained in the country to which they will be assigned—for example, Korea.

An order of missionary sisters, the Poor Clares of the Blessed Sacrament, was founded in Cuernavaca in 1951 and already counts 400 members. It has sent missionaries to Japan, Indonesia, Nigeria, Sierra Leone, and Costa Rica. Invited by the bishop of Novo Redondo (Angola), a group of 17 Poor Clares left their Mexican convent in 1978 to found a convent in that diocese.

Colombia

For more than fifty years, Colombia has shown its concern for mission *ad extra*. The oldest missionary institute in Latin America, the Xaverian Missionaries of Yarumal, was founded there in 1927. When Bishop Angelo Builes (bishop of Santa Rosa de Osos) revealed his plans to open this institute, the other bishops judged that local needs took precedence over the sending of priests and sisters abroad. They still argued this way during the Second Vatican Council. Today the institute counts 168 members, among them 115 priests. Members are working in poor, mission dioceses of Colombia and also in Africa (e.g., in the diocese of Mahagi, Zaire). Bishop Builes also founded a missionary congregation for women, the Missionary Sisters of St. Theresa.

The *Revista de Misiones*, a bimonthly missionary review, is published by the Pontifical Mission Aid Societies, in cooperation with the bishops' conference and the two missionary institutes mentioned above.

Colombian missionaries, men and women, are working in Japan, China, the Philippines, and in different regions of

Africa. Several Colombian Jesuits are carrying on missionary work in central Africa. Backed by four of his bishops, the archbishop of Medellín decided to open a seminary for the training of Fidei Donum priests who will work in mission territories.

As in several other Latin American countries, the Pontifical Mission Aid Societies are becoming better organized and are beginning to play an active role in missionary animation on the national as well as on the diocesan level.

Brazil

Intense missionary reflection is being carried on in Brazil as well. But we should not forget that there still are enormous mission territories in Brazil itself—in the northern dioceses and in the 44 prelatures of the Amazon region. The apostolate among the 45 million Afro-Brazilians is still very often real missionary work. Much attention is being paid to mission *ad intra*.

Since 1977 the bishops' conference has regularly discussed the Brazilian missionary situation at its assemblies. The dioceses having more personnel and better means at their disposal—those in the south—have decided to aid the "poor" dioceses that are still in a missionary situation. About fifty instances of "twinning" have been recorded so far.

The missionary situation of Brazil was thoroughly examined by the bishops in 1978, and the responsibility for mission *ad extra* was emphasized. The bishops opted to stimulate the missionary consciousness of the entire people of God. The episcopal commission for mission is very active. In 1981 it issued a document on missionary education in the schools.

The national missionary council, created by the bishops' conference, is an organ of reflection and mutual cooperation between the Pontifical Mission Aid Societies, the missionary institutes, and other missionary organizations. They jointly discuss missionary activity in Brazil. Missionary animation is very well integrated into national pastoral planning. In addition to the national missionary council, there are also regional missionary councils.

Several dioceses regularly organize mission congresses. In 1981 and 1982 they were held in view of COMLA II.

The numerous activities of the Pontifical Mission Aid Societies are very much like those in Europe. Mission Sunday is very carefully prepared for. An annual theme is chosen. Promotion material is distributed on a large scale: pictures (5 million), posters, calendars, folders, audiovisual aids.

A delegation of the Pan-African Episcopal Conference met with the Brazilian Episcopal Conference in April 1977 to establish contacts between African and Brazilian churches. On that occasion they discussed the feasibility of exchanging missionaries. Brazilian missionaries are now working in Africa. And with its 17 percent black population, Brazil is an appropriate field for African missionaries.

More and more attention is being paid to mission *ad extra*. Brazil intends very consciously to become an evangelizing country. In the past, most missionaries working abroad were unknown to their local church because they were members of international religious institutes or of Brazilian congregations. The well-known Brazilian congregation of the Missionary Sisters of Jesus Crucified, which counts about 1,300 members, has been sending missionaries to Angola and other African nations since 1977. On account of their common language, Angola and Mozambique are appropriate fields for the missionary activity of Brazilians.

An inquiry made by the Pontifical Mission Aid Societies on the number of *ad extra* missionaries reveals that there are more than 600 of them and every year about 30 additional missionaries are being sent out. The Pontifical Mission Aid Societies try to get in touch with them and establish contact between missionaries and their dioceses of origin. In Brasilia, a preparatory course has been organized for missionaries who will be sent *ad extra*.

During his visit to Brazil, John Paul II pointed to the missionary vocation of Brazil and the other Latin American nations. In his address to the CELAM delegates at Rio de Janeiro, July 2, 1980, he said: "May the Lord grant that you may extend the sending out of missionaries in your own countries and to other continents too." During his visit to Manaus on July 10, he referred to the local churches of the Amazon region as "outstandingly missionary" and he added:

Lord, in the presence of your missionary church, I want to praise in a very special way the missions and the missionaries in general—that is, the bishops, the priests, the religious, and the laity....
In this missionary church, I realize that, in virtue of the pontifical office that has been entrusted to me by a secret decree of God, I am the first one responsible for missionary activity.... I want to stimulate and encourage you in your missionary commitment.... Be true evangelizers. According to the stimulating perspective of *Evangelii Nuntiandi* true evangelization is essentially the explicit proclamation of Jesus Christ, the Redeemer of humankind, and of his good news of salvation.

He praised the bishops and their fellow workers for their dedication to the poor and for their gospel proclamation adapted to local cultures.

Other Latin American Countries

In 1981 the Combonian Fathers opened a center for missionary information and conscientization in Quito, Ecuador. They also publish a missionary review, *Iglesias sin Fronteras*.

The recently founded missiological center in Argentina will contribute to the promotion of missionary consciousness. For several years now, Argentina has had a missionary review, *Anales de la Propagación de la Fe*.

The Peruvian Association for Missionaries was founded in 1975. Some of its members are priests and sisters, but most are lay persons. Their first official mission started in the Andes. They are also thinking about *ad extra* mission.

It is impossible to tell exactly how many Latin American missionaries are working in other continents. Statistics are very often lacking. It is only lately that attention has been paid to mission *ad extra*. Most Latin American missionaries are in Africa. Usually they have gone there as members of international religious institutes. The Franciscan Missionaries of Mary, who have 509 Latin American members (from 10 different countries), have sent several sisters to Africa. Brazilian, Mexican,

Colombian, and Uruguayan missionaries are working in Angola.

The Role of Puebla

Latin American evangelization was seriously reflected upon at Medellín. The CELAM meeting in Puebla added the *ad extra* dimension to that reflection. Evangelization was considered in its broad sense. Between Medellín and Puebla, in other words, there occurred an evolution in missionary thinking, which had been prepared for by Medellín's open and universal ecclesiology. Puebla proved that, like the churches of Africa and Asia, the Latin American church, rather than being evangelized, wants to become evangelizing. The church of Latin America has become conscious of the role it can play in the universal church. Its missionary responsibility acquires a world dimension. A new missionary era has begun for Latin America.

Puebla discussed both *ad intra* and *ad extra* evangelization. The first was dealt with on the basis of an analysis of the Latin American missionary situation itself. It became quite clear that in Latin America there are many ethnic groups for whom missionary evangelization is far from being completed; for some it has not even begun. These groups are the Amerindians (36 million), the Afro-Americans (at least 75 million; perhaps as many as 95 million), the Asian-Americans (5 million).

However, evangelization *ad intra* must go together with evangelization *ad extra*. The Puebla final document states:

> The more deeply we are converted to Christ, the more intensely we are drawn by his universal desire for salvation. Likewise, the more alive a local church is, the more it will render the universal church visibly present and the stronger will be its missionary approach to other peoples [n. 363, in *Puebla and Beyond*, John Eagleson and Philip Scharper, eds. (Maryknoll, N.Y.: Orbis, 1979)].

Another passage refers even more explicitly to the *ad extra* missionary task:

The time has come for Latin America to intensify works of mutual service between local churches and to extend them beyond their own frontiers *"ad gentes."* True, we ourselves are in need of missionaries; but we must give from our own poverty. By the same token, our churches have something original and important to offer all: their sense of salvation and liberation, the richness of their peoples' religiosity, the experiences of the CEBs [basic ecclesial communities], their flourishing diversity of ministries, and their hope and joy rooted in the faith. We have already undertaken missionary efforts; these can now be deepened and should be expanded.

We cannot fail to say thanks for the generous help of the universal church and our sister churches. We ask them to stay with us, particularly in the work of training native pastoral agents. In this way we will find ourselves continually fortified for the task of assuming our more universal commitment. And we will also be more capable of an adequate response in serving our own local church [nn. 368–69].

And Puebla did not fail to think about practical implementation:

We must arouse, promote, and give direction to missionary vocations, envisioning centers or seminaries for this specialized purpose [n. 891].

Puebla, therefore, very clearly insists on a breakthrough of mission *ad extra*. As a matter of fact the church of Latin America is so self-confident, so truly a church, and so full of life that it *must* share its vitality with others. However, it will still take some time before all the bishops, priests, religious, and lay persons are fully imbued with this awareness.

The Lima Document

A group of bishops, priests, and religious met in Lima from February 4 to 6, 1981, to further reflect on the declarations of Puebla with regard to mission. The final document of this meeting gives a summary of the views of some mission-minded groups of Latin America's church. Following is a summary of the document:

- A situational analysis reveals that *ad intra* evangelization remains an urgent and very important task.
- The Vatican II teaching on the universal church, and on the collegial responsibility of the particular churches for the evangelization of the world, compels us to conclude that the church of Latin America must open itself up to world mission. However, we must not confine ourselves to *ad intra* evangelization; it must evolve into *ad extra* evangelization.

By the end of the century 80 percent of the world population will be non-Christian. At present, the Latin American church counts 40 percent of all Catholics; by the end of the century it will amount to 50 percent. Hence, our responsibility for world evangelization continues to increase as well. Our contribution will be a blessing for our own local churches. The more we give, the more vocations we will have for *ad intra* evangelization. A church turned upon itself runs the danger of shriveling and of losing its dynamism. Lack of universal openness is one of the causes of our lack of vocations. It is only when a church carries the good news abroad that it becomes mature and dynamic. There is no contradiction between receiving foreign missionaries and sending one's own missionaries *ad extra*.

- We notice that so far Latin America has no missionary consciousness for *ad extra* mission. The few missionaries who were sent out remain unknown and marginal. The ordinary faithful seem to be more receptive of the missionary spirit than the priest. Hence, the great value of awakening a missionary consciousness in the basic communities.

Various causes explain the lack of missionary consciousness. We became accustomed to receiving large-scale outside help, both in personnel and in means. Consequently, we were not sufficiently concerned about self-reliance. During the past decades we were especially worried about *ad intra* evangelization—which, alas, is still badly needed. But being too anxious about our own problems, we neglected *ad extra* mission. Moreover, in former times evangelization was so superficial that a missionary spirit could not possibly develop. Finally, because practically all

Latin American mission territories were entrusted to foreign missionaries, no missionary consciousness was developed among our own bishops, priests, and religious. Fortunately, this situation is changing today.

- The separation in our dioceses between pastoral activity and missionary activity has also prevented the breakthrough of a generalized missionary consciousness. There is no integration of missionary pastoral ministry into diocesan pastoral ministry. The activities of the Pontifical Mission Aid Societies and of the religious institutes are not sufficiently integrated into the life of the local church. Evangelization *ad intra* and evangelization *ad extra* must form a whole in the life of our Christian concomitance. The second is an inseparable concomitant of the first. Both have the same aim: the desire to go to the poorest of the poor, wherever they may be; the urge to share with others the Latin American experience of Jesus Christ the Redeemer. Mission *ad extra* must be considered the fulness of Christian experience. Missionary animation must, then, be a normal dimension of the diocesan pastoral ministry. It must reach all sectors of the people of God.

- The church of Latin America has exceptional advantages for the work of evangelization. Unlike the Western contribution to evangelization during past centuries, the Latin American contribution will not be tied to colonialism and imperialism. It will be a mission of poor countries to poor countries and with poor means. Latin American missionaries can leave for Asia and Africa without any display of power, any superiority complex. Relying on their own Latin American experience, they can offer something original when bringing the good news: their option for the poor; their dedication to justice, liberation, and fellowship; their respect for a people's culture; their model of a popular church with its popular religiosity, in which culture and religion are closely interwoven. Latin American *ad intra* evangelization offers a model for *ad extra* evangelization in Africa and Asia—for example, regarding dialogue with non-Christian religions. It is quite possible that in the future Latin American missionaries will be the most suited evangelizers for Asia and Africa.

- We can send missionaries to Asia, Africa, and the Spanish-speaking parts of the U.S.A. From there they should call upon us to supply yet more missionaries. People gladly believe that we have much to offer with regard to theological insights and pastoral experiences, but they still believe that we cannot afford to supply personnel.

- Church history teaches that a missionary movement often took birth in churches tried and persecuted at home. This was the case in Europe after the French Revolution (and we might add, thus it is today in Poland). Thanks to the situation of conflict in which they live, the Latin American churches are prepared to become *ad extra* evangelizers.
- The commitment of foreign missionaries to Latin America should have more and more a short-term character, so as to allow our churches to rely on themselves. Missionaries must be sent out to territories where their presence is needed for the growth of a local church. Mission must adhere to its "itinerant" nature.
- Mission ought to be declericalized. It is a task of the whole people of God. The grass roots must become missionary and support mission. Missionary vocations must be promoted among the laity.

Mission has been too exclusively entrusted to missionary institutes. It must become the concern of the whole people of God. The bishops, with their priests and religious, are, together with their flock, responsible for mission. The Pontifical Mission Aid Societies and the missionary institutes are their instruments, not their substitutes. Missionaries leave their country, not only to follow a personal vocation but, because called and sent by their community, they enable it to fulfill its missionary obligation.

CHAPTER FIVE

FINAL CONSIDERATIONS

At this point of my survey I wish to add some further considerations and point out the consequences they may have for mission, missionaries, and mission institutes.

Findings

Mission Vocations in the Third Church

Statistics on young missionary candidates in the third church reveal that the time is approaching when the third church will be sending out more young missionaries than will the Western church. A decade from now Western missionaries will probably no longer outnumber non-Western missionaries.

We do not know whether the missionary impulse will revive among Western youth. However, there are reasons to believe that in the years to come the Western churches will overcome their interior crisis and their missionary fatigue. But the Western missionary monopoly or predominance will surely come to an end, if only because the center of gravity within the church is moving toward the third church.

It is surely a fortunate and hopeful sign that from now on evangelization will be borne by all the churches. As in the first centuries the whole church will be missionary. Walbert Bühlmann writes:

> When we speak about a mission crisis—in view of the regression of missionary vocations among us—we should not forget

that this is a Western phenomenon. Today the church as a whole is more missionary than ever before. I should even dare to say that our missionary crisis has been a providential necessity in order to put an end to our missionary monopoly and to give all churches a chance and an impulse to carry out missionary activity [*Evangelisation in der Dritten Welt. Anstösse für Europa*, Freiburg, 1981, p. 18].

The third church is now providing more mission personnel. The Lord's mandate, "Go, therefore, and make of all nations my disciples" (Matt. 28:19; Mark 16:15), was too easily thought of as an impossible task, a utopia. Christians would always be in the minority, we thought. We had to aim at a qualitative rather than a quantitative spreading of the gospel. The arguments used to defend this view were more often sociological than theological. Maybe the future will prove that this attitude reveals a lack of faith in the power of the gospel. World evangelization is not only a human but a divine undertaking. As a matter of fact, the third church is more optimistic than our churches are about the possibility of evangelizing the nations. The expansion of Islam, whose number of adherents is progressively nearing that of Catholics, compels us to serious reflection. If Muslims are concerned about the spreading of their faith, why not Christians also?

More than ever before, *ad gentes* mission is an unfinished task. Catholics (784 million) constitute but 18 percent of the world population (4.4 billion). All Christians together account for 28 percent. The percentage of Christians is declining: by the end of the century only one-fourth, or even less, of the world population (6 billion) will be Christian. The population explosion reaches its highest percentages in non-Christian Asia.

It is legitimate to hope that more personnel will be available for mission once the whole church commits itself to evangelization. But there are other important factors that also point to a bright future for Christian mission.

Advantages of Third World Evangelization

For the first time in recent mission history, we can proceed with a mission liberated from all ties with colonial domination.

Final Considerations

In past centuries Christianity was the religion of colonizers. In time and space evangelization coincided with colonization. Intentionally or not, missionary activity was linked with Western political and cultural domination. In many nations, especially in Asia—for example, in Japan and China—mission was suspect because of this link. It became a serious handicap for conversion. At times it provoked severe persecution.

Decolonization freed Christian mission from this incubus, though not quite completely. Colonialism has its offshoots—neocolonialism. The West retains its economic, technical, and military supremacy, which even today continues to throw dark shadows over the Western missionary presence.

Third World missionaries can present themselves without any display of supremacy, without a superiority complex. There is a strong sense of solidarity between Third World countries in forming a front against Western domination. Hence, Third World missionaries are more likely to be accepted than are Westerners.

Another favorable element for mission of today and tomorrow is the fact that, for the first time in centuries, the gospel can be preached without its Western cultural embodiment. It is being adapted to the cultural, social, and religious context of diverse peoples. Christianity was rejected in many countries, especially in Asia, because of its alien character. Conversion meant alienation. In the past, missionaries as well as colonizers were convinced of the superiority of Western civilization. They believed that they were rendering a great service to "uncivilized" non-Christian peoples by allowing them to enjoy the benefits of Western civilization. Christianity was transplanted together with Western civilization. Evangelization occurred without interreligious or intercultural dialogue.

According to Vatican II such dialogue is an essential aspect of evangelization. Evangelization implies incarnation. Vatican II could never have attained these insights without the contribution of the young churches.

The cultural and religious integration of the good news of the kingdom of God will be taken for granted by missionaries from Third World churches, where the incarnation of the gospel is already in progress.

Once Third World missionaries fully participate in the work

of evangelization, it will no longer be possible to accuse Christianity of being a foreign religion, "the religion of whites," or an alienating religion. They will prove that the gospel is intended for all peoples and that Christ is the Savior of all humankind.

Adaptation and Integration

Inculturation, indigenization, and localization are indispensable aspects of evangelization. They represent a duty accruing to Western as well as Third World missionaries. Integrating oneself into another people's world of living and thinking, assimilating its language and customs, sharing its needs, is difficult, and cannot be achieved without *kenosis* and a spirit of poverty and receptivity.

We are all aware of the usual criticisms made against the approach of Western missionaries of the past: together with the spreading of Western civilization, they transplanted a Western church model, liturgy, catechesis, morality, and pastoral methods. Evangelization was inspired by the ecclesiology and the mentality of their time.

Vatican II insisted on the need for a proclamation of the good news respectful of inculturation, interreligious dialogue, and commitment for a better world. The gospel must appeal to the global context of life. God and humankind are the two poles of evangelization.

In the postconciliar period, most Western missionaries readily adopt the teachings of the council and are eager to incarnate the gospel and to localize their churches. In these matters, they are sometimes more progressive than are indigenous priests.

But there are limits to one's possibilities of adaptation and integration. For a Westerner it will remain difficult, if not impossible, to enter fully into a non-Western mode of feeling and thinking. Only Africans will succeed in creating an African liturgy and an African Christianity. Only Indians will be able to form Christian communities in which the converted Hindu will feel at home.

No matter how much Westerners want to integrate themselves, they remain Western in their behavior, their judgments, their work methods. They cannot easily modify their sense of efficiency, organization, order, punctuality.

Western missionaries are not sufficiently aware of leaving a strongly secularized and desacralized world to move into a deeply religious society in which religion, culture, and everyday life are closely integrated. They come from a world where religion and life, church and state, are separated. In the past they unconsciously transplanted this dualism to Africa, Asia, Oceania. Third World peoples have since reprimanded missionaries for this mistake. They ask them to respect their religiosity, their sacred rites and symbols, their feelings and bodily expression. They respond to a proclamation of the Christian faith respectful of the unity between religion and life, a proclamation that appeals to their entire life.

Evangelization cannot be fully successful unless Christianity acquires a popular character. The Spanish and Portuguese missionaries of the sixteenth and seventeenth centuries can be accused of having been too much tied to colonial domination, but coming from a world where religion and life were one, where religion still had a thoroughly popular character, they promoted the birth of a popular Christianity in Latin America. Recent studies in Latin American popular religiosity help us discover flaws in missionary methods. Missionaries of the nineteenth and twentieth centuries paid very little attention to the popular character of religion. This mistake partly explains the birth of so many independent Christian churches and sects, especially in Africa, where they count 15 million adherents.

Thanks to their religious background, Third World missionaries will easily commit themselves to foster a popular Christianity, to integrate the gospel in the global human reality. They will spontaneously respect the valuable elements they find in religious traditions and needs. Inculturation does not stop at esteem for strictly cultural realities; it also includes appreciation of religious values, for religion and culture are closely interrelated.

It would, however, be a mistake to think that, arriving in a mission area, Third World missionaries need not exert any effort to leave behind their own people, to question their own opinions and customs, to distance themselves from their own local pastoral methods, to listen, to receive, and to get to know the people's social situation, before judging and acting. Now and then Latin American missionaries are accused of merely transplanting their own local church models and pastoral methods. At times the same criticism is made against the approach of young Polish missionaries.

We must take into account that Third World churches, which have only recently opened up to mission *ad extra*, have no in-depth experience as yet regarding evangelization, an undertaking that even today remains very demanding. The best means for preparing missionaries for their task are often lacking. This is not the case for the members of international missionary institutes; they can rely on the institute's long years of experience, an appropriate preparation, and adequate assistance in the mission field. Fidei Donum priests and lay missionaries generally do not enjoy such favorable conditions.

Insofar as they are closer to the ones they evangelize, Third World missionaries are in a privileged position in comparison with Westerners. They have a better understanding of a Third World culture, religious traditions, and needs. In fact, coming from a developing country, they should also be closer to the masses as regards their socio-economic conditions. Better than Western missionaries, they should be acquainted with the problems of poverty. They should be inclined to be not only "for" and "with" the poor, but to live "as" the poor and to commit themselves to social justice for them. But is this borne out in reality? It is a delicate and difficult question. Given its great importance, it cannot be dismissed.

We should not forget that most Third World peoples are poor, oppressed, exploited, marginalized. We refer today, as never before, to the church of the poor, to the evangelical predilection for the poor, to the option for the poor. The church of Latin America gives us an example in this regard. Lately, general chapters of religious institutes have also dealt at length with the option for the poor.

Yet we observe that among the clergy of Third World countries there is often a great difference between declarations of poverty and the practice of poverty. In terms of their mentality, their way of life, and things they surround themselves with, church leaders, priests, and religious often belong to the bourgeoisie, to the intellectual class, or the well-off. Hence, they are alienated from the masses of the people. Not so long ago this same situation prevailed in Europe.

Of course, the option for the poor should not be exclusive. We need also a pastoral ministry for the so-called elites. But in countries where the majority of the people are poor, the church must first of all be a church of the poor and defend their rights. It must be a prophetic church. This is a demand of evangelical charity, but also of inculturation, taken in its broadest sense. It is not enough to become one with others' religious traditions and with their culture in the narrow sense; we must also be one with them in their socio-economic situation. The poor have a culture of their own.

Everybody knows how many bishops, priests, religious, and lay persons, especially in Latin America, risk their lives in identifying themselves with the poor in their struggle for justice.

To be faithful to the charismatic character of their vocation, religious must be the vanguard of a prophetic church. The Congregation of Religious and Secular Institutes made this very clear in its Instruction of August 12, 1980.

A "church of the poor" calls for "religious of the poor." Third World religious and missionaries should make an examination of conscience regarding their attitude toward the poor. It might lead to painful decisions.

This is a very real problem for international religious institutes with members in the Third World. Usually the superiors of these institutes want to avoid all forms of discrimination among the members—for example, regarding clothing, food, lodging, equipment, studies, and the like. Consequently, all members adopt a Western way of life. This is very often the desire, if not the claim, of members from Third World countries. Speaking as an African, President Julius Nyerere of Tanzania can tell priests and missionaries that the gospel asks them to live close to the people and as much as possible like them. The superiors of international institutes, most of them whites, can hardly make such demands. What makes the problem still more complex is the fact that white missionaries are frequently unable to abandon their Western way of life.

Fortunately, more and more Third World priests, religious, and missionaries are convinced that their training, their spirituality, and their way of life must be determined by the socio-economic situation of the people.

Without doubt, one must make a distinction between socioeconomic poverty, an evil, and evangelical poverty, a gospel demand. Yet the practice of evangelical poverty calls for participation in the fate of the poor among whom we live. It is a way of contributing to their human liberation and promotion. This view is increasingly gaining ground in the Third World.

I have selected a few witnesses from northern India. Latin America too can provide many such testimonies (see Leonardo Boff, *God's Witnesses in the Heart of the World* [Chicago: Claret Center for Resources in Spirituality, 1981]).

In 1981 and 1982 the bishops and rectors of the major seminaries of the Hindi region repeatedly dealt with the problem of seminary training. Poverty was one of their main concerns. They formulated the following considerations:

We can no longer be merely for the poor. Today we have to be the church of the poor. But the question that has been bothering me for many years is whether we really mean what we say. Can a church that is really the church of the poor . . . in a country like India, where millions are below the poverty line, really afford the type of seminaries we now have? Are not these a monumental evidence that we are the church of the affluent? Are we not members of some sort of Rotary Club or Lions Club who live comfortably but still organize some sort of relief for the poor? Is not the ease with which we put up buildings, buy new equipment, plan out study tours, organize all sorts of seminars, going against all that we proclaim? Are we not telling the poor by our lives that we have a bottomless pool of funds? Are not our concepts of scholarship and research, standards of efficiency, culture and leisure, etc., taken over from affluent countries? If a priest is expected to be a "man of pastoral compassion," then he must share in the hardships of his people, he must live close to them; and yet, joining the clerical circle seems to have the opposite effect. Hence, it should not surprise anybody if seminarians who are used to large structures, comfortable rooms, sufficient money to meet their expenses, find it difficult to adjust themselves to working in rural areas [Subhash Anand, "Training Priests for North India," *Vidyajyoti*, Jan. 1982, pp. 32–44].

Indian Jesuits working in northern India have come to the same insights for the training of their young missionaries. According to them, this training should not only be determined by theological principles about the religious life, but also by the socio-economic situation of the people to whom the missionaries will dedicate their lives. Instead, they have been trained to live according to the standards of a cultural elite and an elitist society. This "elitization" has alienated them from their own families, their own people, and their own culture. The lifestyle of these elites is Western. Hence, the mode of life in the training houses does not prepare the young to fit into the social context of the people they want to serve. Their prayer life offers but little room for the painful reality of the suffering of the masses with whom they live. Mentally they no longer belong to the world of the poor. This elitist formation can persist thanks to Western financial aid.

In India, as in Africa, many candidates abhor manual labor. Yet it is a way to share the ordinary life of the people and to contribute somewhat to their own upkeep. In an address to a conference of religious superiors, Indian Bishop J. Saupin, S.J. (Daltonganj), declared:

> There is something that is constantly agitating my mind and my spirit, and that is the formation of our personnel. As we look today at our houses of formation and the attitudes we give our young personnel, I feel that . . . we take them from one pattern of life and put them into another. I would think that in our houses of formation and in the formation techniques and programmes that we have, we build up in our young religious an upper middle-class society mentality. They come to our novitiates and we give them all the facilities, and put them into a cultural bracket that is away from rural poverty. There are experiments, granted, when we send them back to this milieu; but is there a constant commitment to discovery? I really wonder   [J. Velamkunnel, "Formation of Religious and Service to the Poor in the Context of North India," *Vidyajyoti*, 44 (1980): 323].

Inculturation of theology, as much as inculturation of religious life, requires that evangelizers integrate both themselves and their message in the culture of the poor. Inculturation is too often conceived of as integration into the culture of an elite. Yet the masses of the poor are the real creators and bearers of the culture of the people. Indigenous theology is not formulated by an elite; it arises from the experience that the poor come to have of Christ. With regard to this problem, Aloysius Pieris, S.J. (Sri Lanka), writes:

> If, however, this last observation is valid, namely, that an indigenous theology in our context is an articulation of the Christ experience of Asia's poor, then neither the clerical leadership of the church nor even the Asian [liberation] theologians who have been educated in an elitist culture can claim to be the engineers of an indigenous theology. In fact, like the hierarchical church, these theologians too speak of the poor in the third person! This is an implicit acknowledgment that they are not really poor. On the other hand, the poor have not yet been truly evangelized and they too are not, therefore, qualified as yet to spell out an indigenous theology for Asia.
>
> The Asian dilemma, then, can be summed up as follows: the theologians are not (yet) poor; and the poor are not (yet) theologians! This dilemma can be resolved only in the local churches of Asia, i.e., in the grassroots communities where the theologians and the poor become culturally reconciled through a process of mutual evangelization (SEDOS, April 1, 1982, pp. 104–5).

Here we can also refer to a paragraph of the final declaration of the sixth Symposium of Episcopal Conferences of Africa and Madagascar (Yaoundé, June 29 to July 5, 1981), which dealt with "Justice and Evangelization in Africa":

> How could we possibly invite the country's elite to accept a sober lifestyle, adapted to the concrete reality of our nations, if we allow ourselves to be tempted and seduced by foreign models that far exceed the possibilities of the mass of our fellow citizens? [n.17].

This is undoubtedly a delicate problem. Third World priests and religious find it hard to resist the fascination of the Western way of life. The international religious institutes, trying to avoid any form of discrimination, advocate some kind of uniformity in their way of life and their spirituality, so as to promote fellowship and solidarity.

A training program aimed at identification with the poor cannot be imposed. Third World religious must themselves come to the conclusion that fidelity to their own people calls for a way of life different from that of their Western coreligious.

Some international religious institutes send some young candidates from the Third World to be trained in Europe or in North America. They should consider whether training abroad should not be reserved rather to members who have already found their identity and have achieved a certain degree of maturity.

A Deepened and Renewed Vision of Mission

It becomes evident from the 1974 synod of bishops that the contribution of each continent is needed to reach a balanced and complete understanding of the mission of the church. Different insights complement each other. So it is that the *Evangelii Nuntiandi* view of the church and of mission is much richer than that of previous major mission encyclicals. All cultures, religions, and human situations must come into contact with the gospel. Only then will it be grasped in all its depth and breadth.

The churches must exchange with one another their reflections on the faith. Formerly the churches of different countries, or even of the same country, used to live side by side with but very little intercommunication. And the universal church was divided in two blocs: the old, established churches and the "fledgling" or mission churches. Vatican II has taught us to look at the church as a worldwide communion of equal local churches that, living in a bond of close communion, cooperation, and exchange, share one another's joys and needs, and are jointly responsible for the mission of the one church. Universality, solidarity, reciprocity have become inseparable dimensions of interchurch relationships.

This solidarity is also reflected in our ever more unified world, characterized by the constant development of various forms of interdependence, intercultural exchange, and mutual contacts.

The pastoral reflection carried on in the Latin American church should be a source of inspiration for church upbuilding in Africa. In this way Africans could discover certain flaws in their methods of evangelization—for example, an inadequate option for the poor. Africa, Asia, Latin America, Oceania, and the West all have something to learn from each other.

As a matter of fact, horizontal communication between the continents has been rather poor. How much do the bishops of Asia and Africa know about Latin American church problems and ecclesial renewal? And vice versa. Communication remains very much vertically directed—from South to North, from the Third World to the West and to Rome.

Fortunately, horizontal communication has commenced. The synod of bishops is an excellent instrument for interchurch reflection and exchange. Other initiatives and organizations promote interchurch dialogue—for example, the Ecumenical Association of Third World Theologians (EATWOT), the congresses of international organizations, and the like.

Obviously, the international missionary institutes can play an important role in promoting interchurch exchange and service. They help local churches to transcend their tendency to close in upon themselves. Thanks to the international spreading of their members, they establish contacts between one local church and several other churches. They stimulate the exchange of personnel and spiritual values. Thus the churches begin to evangelize one another. The former one-way mission is replaced by "reverse mission." Consequently, the international religious institutes are excellent instruments for promoting reciprocity between the churches.

In bringing together members from different countries, cultures, and continents, the international institutes enrich themselves. Members from North and South, East and West, share their understanding and experience of the faith, their spirituality, their views on missionary methods, as well as their mentality, their traits, their work methods. In this way they can enrich one another and help one another with their shortcomings. Third World religious sometimes keep on working without taking time to reflect on their work. At times they are careless and rather inefficient. But the Western rational and analytic way of thinking has its dangers too: it tends to neglect feeling and intuition, to build up unrealistic theories, to separate what should only be distinguished. It becomes unable to reconcile the various elements of one and the same reality and creates problems where there are none. It is less difficult for the Third World mind than for the Western mind to perceive the unity between faith and life, prayer and action, evangelization and development, theology and spirituality. The Third World might tend to overlook the human person and human freedom, but thanks to a stronger community spirit it is not subject to the evils of Western individualism. Coexistence and collaboration of Westerners with non-Westerners can help the former to develop a community spirit and the latter to appreciate more the individual human person.

The number of Western missionaries is decreasing everywhere. Some local bishops and priests give the impression of longing for the moment when the last Western missionary will be gone. Others, on the contrary, maintain that the presence of foreign, including Western, missionaries will always be desirable, even when sufficient local personnel will be on hand. The Western churches must continue to send out a sufficient number of missionaries. The young churches need the contribution of the Western churches, which occupy a privileged position thanks to their twenty centuries of reflection on and experience of the faith. The presence of Western missionaries will always be a blessing for Third World churches.

Internationalization of Mission Personnel

In a world where communication between peoples, countries, and churches becomes more and more intense and universal, mission must also develop an interchurch, supranational, and worldwide dimension.

The time of the "national" mission has gone—that is, of mission territories that, for political reasons, were entrusted to missionaries of the colonizing power. The missions of the Belgian Congo were entrusted to Belgian missionaries, those of *La*

France d'outre-mer to French missionaries. In their mission encyclicals, Benedict XV and Pius XI had still to rebuke some missionaries for their exaggerated nationalism. Colonialism has now come to an end. Neocolonialism, very much criticized, will also disappear one day. Pius XII pointed repeatedly to the supranational character of mission. Nationalism, of which missionaries were often guilty, is now considered senseless. Today missionaries are world citizens, servants of the universal church, without forgetting, however, that they are at the same time envoys of their local churches.

The former *jus commissionis*, by which the evangelization of some territories was entrusted exclusively to a given missionary institute, has become pointless in the ecclesial context of today.

Missionaries from different nations should be sent out to the same country, if political conditions do not prevent it. Their diversity is a living sign of the unity in pluriformity of the universal church.

More than ever before, the missionary policy of the Sacred Congregation for the Evangelization of Peoples should be worked out on a world level. It must be concerned about an efficient spreading of missionary personnel and financial aid. Hence it is essential to ensure a close cooperation between this congregation and the international mission institutes, the most adequate means for an efficient and international allocation of missionaries. They give a supranational character to mission.

Missionary institutes are working more and more with international teams, symbols of universal fellowship in Christ, of the universality of the gospel, and of the church's catholicity and respect for every race and culture. The Jesuits, the White Fathers, and others have been doing this for a long time.

Unlike the often nationalist Western mission of previous times, Third World mission has had, from the very start, an international character. Third World missionaries are not only sent out to various countries; most of the time they are also working in international teams.

With regard to the universal spreading and mixing of all nationalities, there is probably no religious institute that has been so radical, and for so many years, as the Franciscan Missionaries of Mary. Of the 9,056 members, 4,818 are from Europe, 2,706

Final Considerations 85

from Asia, 662 from North America, 509 from Latin America, 265 from Africa, and 96 from Australia. The members are allocated as follows:

- In Africa 908 sisters from 18 countries are at work. Of their 265 African sisters (12 nationalities), 26 are stationed outside Africa. Among the 908 sisters in Africa, there are 588 Europeans, 239 Africans, 37 Asians, 32 North Americans, 7 Oceanians, and 5 Latin Americans.
- In Asia there are 2,965 sisters from 18 countries, including 2,562 Asian sisters (from India, 1,226; Japan, 364; the Philippines, 241; China, 211; Sri Lanka, 106; Vietnam, 58; other countries, 356); 144 of the 2,706 Asian members are working in other continents. The number of Asian sisters shows that the future of the congregation lies in that continent. The 2,965 sisters working in Asia come from Asia, Europe (340), Africa (6), North America (43), Oceania (10), and Latin America (4).
- There are 966 sisters in Latin America. Of the 509 Latin American sisters (10 nationalities), 21 are working outside Latin America. The sisters stationed in Latin America come from Latin America (483), Europe (440), North America (18), Africa (2), Asia (21), and Oceania (2).
- In Oceania 144 sisters are at work. There are 96 local sisters, all from Australia; 20 of them have left for other continents. Besides the Australian sisters (71), there are also European (45), Asian (12), and North American (16) sisters working there.
- The congregation has 3,459 sisters in Europe. Of the 4,818 European sisters (22 nationalities), 1,468 are working in other continents. Besides the Europeans, sisters from all other continents are working in Europe.
- In North America 614 sisters from various continents are at work; 125 of the 662 North American sisters are working outside the U.S.A. and Canada.

The extremely international and mixed involvement of the members creates problems that should not be neglected. Members need a transcultural formation program. They must be prepared to transcend their own culture, to integrate themselves into the culture of the country where they will work and live with coreligious from other countries and cultures. This readiness is part of the spirituality of all members, even of those who are stationed in their own country. Differences regarding language, culture, and habits can be so great within the same continent that, for example, an Asian will feel as much a stranger in another Asian country as will a European.

The spreading of personnel in international teams should not be an obstacle to the personality development of the members, nor should it lead to loneliness for lack of contact with compatriots. Frequent transfers could have the harmful effect that a missionary never gets to know the language, the culture, the habits, and the problems of a local population. Internationalization has its limits.

International missionary institutes should without any doubt promote an international spirit among their members. Every member must feel at home in the institute and be available for its universal commitment. All members are equal. Discrimination and racism must be avoided. Yet this raises some problems. Western international institutes are used to following a Western way of life, and they have transplanted themselves as such in the Third World. I have already mentioned that, even for the sake of equality, it would be a mistake to offer all members a training and a lifestyle inspired by the Western way of life. Another danger, related to this one, consists in searching for and propagating a standard model of, for example, a Jesuit, a Franciscan, a White Father, a Franciscan Missionary of Mary Sister. This model would undoubtedly be of Western inspiration.

The internationalization of the institutes must be adapted to the process of inculturation and diversification within the universal church. Just as the African, Asian, and Latin American churches are growing, so there must develop a model of priest, religious, and missionary adapted to the economic and sociocultural context of each continent. Before feeling "internationally," the members of the international institutes must be able to think, feel, and live "nationally." They must first be allowed to be themselves among their own people.

We need typically African and typically Indian missionaries. An African Holy Spirit Father will be different from a French one, and an Indian Jesuit will be different from a European Jesuit.

Only in this way will the African, Asian, and Latin American members make a positive contribution to an institute's spirituality, mode of life, and methods of working.

International missionary institutes must, therefore, undergo a metamorphosis. Their spirituality, their rule, their methods of working must be freed from their exclusively Western character, in order to build a community in which members from Third World churches can be themselves and in their own way be faithful to their vocation. But being oneself is not synonymous with particularism. It is impossible to live in an international community without a minimum of *kenosis*, without universal openness.

Today the general chapters of the international institutes are challenged to be future-oriented. They must ask themselves how the institute's composition regarding nationalities will evolve during the next decade. If they have the courage to draw the necessary conclusions, it is quite probable that metamorphosis will become their main concern.

International and Local Mission Institutes

As can be gathered from the previous chapters, in Third World churches involvement for mission *ad extra* is still mainly the work of international missionary institutes. Yet, this must not be an obstacle to the foundation of local missionary societies. In fact the international missionary institutes should promote such foundations, as the Combonian Fathers are doing in East Africa, and the M.E.P. Fathers in Vietnam and elsewhere. For the good of the church and of its mission, it is necessary that indigenous African and Asian missionary institutes, with or without vows, be founded; in their turn, they can become international. The Sisters and the Brothers of Mother Teresa are giving an example in this matter.

It is fitting, nevertheless, that international missionary institutes implant themselves and recruit members in the young churches. By allowing these churches to benefit from their long missionary experience and from the advantages of a well-organized commitment, those institutes help young churches to become missionary *ad extra* as quickly and as efficiently as possible. Thus right from the start, the missionary dedication of these churches acquires a universal dimension. In some countries international institutes have already lost their Western external outlook and have become indigenous thanks to the large number of local members. This is the case, for example, in India.

The exclusively missionary institutes founded for mission *ad extra* ought to ask themselves whether they can accept members for evangelization *ad intra*. My study on the rise of missionary awareness in Third World churches reveals that they consider mission *ad extra* a new and special commitment, to which they intend to give a universal character. Only those who are sent out to churches in other countries are given the title "missionary." Third World churches take pride in talking about their missionaries. They have revalidated a title that they might have previously considered to be uncongenial and old-fashioned.

It seems quite appropriate that the exclusively missionary institutes should help Third World churches with regard to mission *ad extra* by limiting themselves to recruiting only members who will serve *ad extra*. At the same time, these institutes remain faithful to their own charism. Mission *ad gentes* usually involves being sent *ad extra*, which implies a transreligious and frequently also a transcultural commitment. This is impossible without a special disposition, a proper spirituality, an adequate training and appropriate methods. It remains a special vocation.

Recently, and as a result of the renewed understanding of mission and the important changes in the missionary context, some missionary institutes have a hard time in defining their objectives and their field of action. Should they be guided by the quite generally accepted understanding of evangelization as "mission on the six continents"? Does the re-evangelization of our Western dechristianized masses belong to the tasks of missionary institutes? These questions are open to endless discussion. No matter what we might think about them, there are sufficient reasons to conclude that, as in previous times, persons and institutes opting for mission *ad gentes* and *ad extra*, and making it their specific vocation, will always be needed.

Evangelization by Established Churches: Unneccesary?

In recent years the question has sometimes been raised, Has the task of missionary institutes not come to an end? Some have claimed that foreign missionaries are no longer needed, once the young churches have their own personnel to carry on the work of evangelization. Consequently, there would be no reason for missionary institutes to go on recruiting new members in Western countries. The mission of the old Christian churches has been fulfilled. Obviously, the propagation of such views had harmful effects on the promotion of missionary vocations.

However, it should have been clear that, according to Vatican II ecclesiology, every local church must be missionary if it intends to be a true church. The loss of missionary dynamism is a symptom of a crisis or of a disease. Becoming missionary *ad extra* is an expression of evangelical authenticity, of inner fulness of life. By becoming missionary in their turn, Third World churches prove that they grasped this truth. It may indeed be humiliating for Western churches to be reminded of their lasting missionary obligation by the churches that are the fruit of their own missionary activity.

It pertains to the missionary institutes' responsibility to safeguard or to reawaken the missionary consciousness of the Western churches, which at all cost must remain missionary *ad extra*. The participation of Third World missionaries in this missionary conscientization is most welcome.

Mission *ad gentes* remains an immense task. In many regions of the world evangelization has just started, and local personnel is still minimal in numbers. More than two-thirds of humankind do not know Christ. The evangelization of the world cannot be carried out by Third World churches alone, without the help of the West. It is therefore nonsense to say that the work of mission has come to an end.

The missionary institutes must realize that today their role is as important as ever before, and that it might even become more important in the future. Their present experience of rejuvenation, by young members coming from third church provinces, should help them regain self-confidence.

The Whole People of God

The data we have considered in this book make it quite clear that the third church is very much concerned about making evangelization a task pertaining to the whole people of God. It is a mission entrusted to the grassroots as well as to the hierarchy, to the laity as well as to the clergy.

It is striking that in several countries the bishops' conferences are the first to speak about mission *ad extra* and that they themselves take the initiative of founding missionary seminaries. This is a consequence of the Vatican II teaching on the bishops' collegial responsibility for world evangelization. In former times, mission was carried out by the popes and religious institutes. The new missionary institutes or missionary works were initiatives of priests, lay persons, or bishops acting on their own. They had a charismatic origin. Today we see that the hierarchy is taking the initiative.

Bishops wish that their churches will become missionary and that evangelizers—priests, religious, lay persons—will be sent out. Most of them give their full support to the religious institutes, even to the international institutes. They consider the missionary institutes instruments in the fulfillment of their missionary task. According to an older ecclesiology, dioceses become missionary by sending out Fidei Donum priests, whereas the missionary institutes were at the service of the pope, he alone being responsible for world mission. Today this responsibility is being borne jointly by the pope and the college of bishops. Missionary institutes, therefore, are to be at the service of the bishops and the bishops' conferences. They are at the service of both the universal church and the local churches.

International missionary institutes must, then, realize that they have also a local, a "national" character. Without losing their relative autonomy and their charismatic character, they should collaborate closely with local bishops and with local episcopal conferences. Missionaries should consider themselves sent by their community of origin and remain in close contact with it, as is asked by *Ad Gentes* (n. 37).

Vatican II strengthened the bonds between the bishops and

the religious institutes (See L.G. nn. 44-45; C.D. nn. 33-35; A.G. n. 31, 32, 38; P.C. n. 23; see also Eccl. Sanctae III, 6, 10, 11). More recent documents come back to this point—for example, the Instruction of the Propaganda Congregation, *Relationes in Territoriis Missionum* (Feb. 24, 1969), the joint Instruction of the Congregation of the Bishops and of the Congregation of Religious, *Mutuae Relationes* (May 14, 1978). *Ad Gentes* (n. 33) insists on a close cooperation between episcopal conferences and conferences of religious superiors. We have already seen that Latin America can be taken as a model of such collaboration.

Since the publication of the encyclical *Fidei Donum* (April 21, 1957), mission is no longer the monopoly of missionary institutes. Bishops take the initiative of sending their own priests, religious, and lay persons to churches in need of personnel. Pius XII as well as his successors encouraged them to do so. In this way the specifically missionary responsibility of bishops and of local churches is emphasized. It also promotes solidarity and reciprocal service between the churches.

However, as mentioned already, experience has taught that the Fidei Donum vocation is a difficult one. The danger of disappointment and failure is very real when preparation, spiritual direction, and financial aid are lacking.

Third World bishops have also started to send out diocesan priests and religious. They should take advantage of the experience of the Western churches in this matter. The difficulties involved in ensuring the needed preparation and animation should inspire prudence. At least for the time being, the institutional commitment of missionaries remains the most appropriate form of dedication.

Conclusion

In their interventions at the 1974 synod of bishops, the Third World bishops spoke enthusiastically about the future of the gospel in their continents. They witnessed to their faith in the power of the Spirit of God, "the principal agent of evangelization" (E.N., n. 75). They were full of hope with regard to evangelization:

> We live in the church at the privileged moment of the Spirit. . . . It is in the evangelizing mission of the church that he is most active [E.N., n. 75].

It has been said that the Acts of the Apostles are being lived over again in the young churches, where the gospel is still radiating in all its newness. The bishops of Asia as well as those of Africa and Latin America spoke in hopeful terms of the future of mission. They pointed to the fatigue, the lack of self-confidence, of many Western churches, which have become so used to the gospel that they no longer experience its newness and its perennial youth. They want to restore self-confidence to the Western churches.

In this study I have spoken in hopeful terms about the Third World churches. To be sure, they have their problems and weaknesses. We know that they face many difficulties. But their faith, their hope, and their vitality, expressed in their becoming missionary churches, is not so well known. And this is what I wanted to stress.

Thanks to the Third World churches, the universal church and its mission can look into the future with great hope. Hence we conclude with the words of Walbert Bühlmann:

> There is far too much talk about crisis in the Church, far too little about the opportunities we are offered. In the course of history, opportunities have always outnumbered the tribulations; if it were not so, the Church would not have survived. The outstanding opportunity of the present time is the coming of a Church which I would like to call the "Third Church," that is to say, the Church of the south as distinct from the Churches of east and west. This coming is an epoch-making event within the one Church of Christ [*The Coming of the Third Church* (Maryknoll, N.Y.: Orbis Books, 1976), p. ix].

INDEX

Abidjan (Ivory Coast), 25
Acts of the Apostles, 92
Ad extra evangelization, definition of, 7
Ad Gentes: compared with *Evangelii Nuntiandi*, 8; on episcopal conferences and conferences of religious superiors, 91; on exchange of diocesan priests, 21; on institutional commitment to mission, 20; on missionaries and their sending communities, 90; on religious and mission, 21; and third church mission, 2-3, 4, 5, 6, 9, 28
Ad gentes mission, definition of, 7
Ad intra evangelization, definition of, 7
Africa, 13; basic ecclesial communties in, 25; Catholic population of, 12, 23-24; Christian population of, 23; independent churches and sects in, 23, 24, 75; indigenous clerical congregations in, 19; missionaries from, 8, 85; missionaries to, 20, 40, 52, 53, 56, 62, 63, 64, 65-66, 85; number of bishops in, 18; number of indigenous religious women in, 30; number of novices in, 18; number of priestly ordinations in, 15; number of priests in, 14; number of seminarians in, 15; number of sisters in, 17; population of, 42; Protestant population of, 23; ratio of population to priests in, 16, 24; and third church on other continents, 32
African Franciscan Missionaries of Mary, 30
Afro-Brasilians, 63
Aggiornamento, 56
All-India Seminar (Bangalore), 9, 45-46
Alokolam (Uganda), 32
Alwaye (India), 44
Amalorpavadass, D. S., 47
Amazon region, 63, 64
AMECEA, 31
AMOR (Asian Meeting of Religious), 37
Anales de la Propagación de la Fe, 65
Anand, Subhash, 78
Angola, 26, 62, 64, 65-66

Apostles of Jesus, 18, 28, 31-32
Argentina, 40, 58-59, 60, 65
Asia: and *ad extra* mission, 34; Catholic population of, 34; missionaries from, 41-42, 85; missionaries to, 41, 52, 53, 85; number of bishops in, 6, 12; number of novices in, 18; number of priestly ordinations in, 15; number of priests in, 14-15, 37; number of seminarians in, 16; number of sisters in, 17, 37; population of, 34; ratio of population to priests in, 16; and third church on other continents, 82
Asian Conference of Major Religious Superiors, 37
Asian Meeting of Religious, 37
Association of Member Episcopal Conferences of Eastern Asia, 31
Augustinians, 29
Australia, 49
Baguio (Philippines), 36, 39
Bangalore (India), 44
Bangalore Conference (All-India Seminar), 9, 45-46
Bangladesh, 56
Bannabikira Sisters, 31
Barrett, D., 23
Basic Christian communities. *See* Basic ecclesial communities
Basic ecclesial communities, 25, 59, 61, 67, 68
Belgian Congo, 83
Belgium, 83
Benares, 46
Benebikira Sisters, 31
Benedictines, 29
Benetereziya Sisters, 27, 31
Benin, 27
Bethlehem Missionaries, 19
Bhutan, 49
Bigard Memorial Seminary (Nigeria), 27
Bishops' Institute for Interreligious Affairs (Asia), 36
Bishops' Institute for Missionary Apostolate (Asia), 36

Bishops' Institute for Social Action (Asia), 36
Boff, Leonardo, 78
Bolivia, 60
Bombay, 37, 64
Brasilia, 61, 64
Brazil, 13, 53, 63; black population of, 64; increase of seminarians in, 59; John Paul II's visit to, 64-65; missionaries from, 64, 65, 66; missionaries to, 30, 40, 49, 52-53
Brazilian Episcopal Conference, 64
British Guyana, 49
Brothers, number of in the world, 17
Buddhism, 34, 43, 56
Buenos Aires, 61
Bühlmann, Walbert, ix, 12, 71-72, 92
Buichu diocese (Vietnam), 54
Builes, Bishop Angelo, 62
Bukinda (Uganda), 32
Burundi, 24, 32; missionaries from, 27; missionaries to, 40
Cameroon, 27, 30, 40
Capuchin Fathers, 14, 28
Caribbean, 40, 49
Carmelites of Mary Immaculate, 18, 45
Cathechesis, 60-61, 74
Catholic Foreign Mission Society of America. *See* Maryknoll
Catholics, number of in the world, 72
CELAM, 10, 58, 59, 60, 61, 64, 66. *See also* Medellín Conference; Puebla Conference
Center for Religion and Society (Sri Lanka), 56
Chad, 27
Chaghua (Taiwan), 36
Chanda (India), 45
Chang, Dr., 50
Chile, 59
China, 16, 34, 73, 85; missionaries to, 62
Choi, Bishop J., 51
Christians, number of in the world, 72
Christus Dominus, 5, 91
C.I.C.M. Fathers: and African countries, 11, 14, 18, 20, 29, 40; and Asian countries, 14, 20, 40; and Caribbean countries, 30, 40; and Europe, 14; indigenization of, 19; and Latin American countries, 20, 30, 40; non-European, 13; and the U.S., 14, 30
Cistercians, 29
CLAR (Conference Latinoamericana de Religiosos), 60, 61
Claretians, 29
Colombia, 59, 60, 63; missionaries from, 62-63, 66
Colombo (Sri Lanka), 37, 56
Colonialism, 58, 69, 72-73

Combonian Fathers, 19, 31, 32-33, 65, 87
Coming of the Third Church, The (Bühlmann), ix, 12, 92
COMLA (Congreso Misionero Latinoamericano), 61
COMLA II, 61, 63
Comunidades de base. *See* Basic ecclesial communities
Congo. *See* People's Republic of the Congo; Belgian Congo
Congregation for the Clergy, 16
Congregation for the Evangelization of Peoples, 17, 84, 91
Congregation of Religious and Secular Institutes, 77, 91
Congregation of the Bishops, 91
Congregation of the Mother Co-Redemptrix, 54
Congregation of the Mother of Carmel, 48
Congreso Misionero Latinoamericano (COMLA), 61, 63
Consolata Society for Foreign Missions, 19
Córdoba (Argentina), 59
Costa Rica, 62
Cotonou (Benin), 27
Cuernavaca (Mexico), 62
Daughters of Charity, 18
Daughters of the Holy Cross, 48
Decolonization, 73
de la Motte, Bishop Pierre Lambert, 1
Diebougou (Upper Volta), 30
Diocesan priests, proportion of religious priests to, 17
Dioceses, number of in the world, 12
Dominican Republic, 40, 59
Dominicans, 29
Eastern-rite Catholics in India, 44-45
EATWOT (Ecumenical Association of Third World Theologians), 82
Ecclesiae Sanctae III, 91
Ecclesiology: of Medellín Conference, 66; and mission, 74; before Vatican II, 90; of Vatican II, 3, 5, 6, 24, 89
Ecuador, 60
Ecumenical Association of Third World Theologians (EATWOT), 82
Ekandem, Cardinal, 28
Episcopal Conference of Brazil, 59
Ethiopia. *See* AMECEA
Europe, 57, 64, 70; Catholic population of, 12; missionaries from, 1, 84, 85; missionaries to, 40, 48, 49, 52, 85; number of dioceses in, 12; number of priestly ordinations in, 15; number of priests in, 15; number of seminarians in, 16; number of sisters in, 17; ratio of population to priests in, 16
Evangelii Nuntiandi: and Japanese mission, 52; John Paul II on, 65; on religious

and mission, 21; third church bishops and, 91-92; and third church mission, 8-9, 24, 81
Evangelisation in der Dritten Welt. Antösse für Europa 5 (Bühlmann), 71-72
Evangelizing Sisters of Mary, 18, 28, 33
FABC, 36, 46, 52. *See also* Taipei Conference
Federation of Asian Bishops' Conference. *See* FABC
Fidei Donum, 11, 21, 26, 91
Fidei Donum priests, 20, 21, 46, 63, 76, 90, 91
Fiji Islands, 46, 49
First World. *See* Western world
Foreign Mission of Paris, 1, 19, 87
France, 84
Franciscan Missionaries of Mary, 19, 40, 48, 53, 65, 84, 85
French Revolution, 70
Gabon, 24, 26
Gambia, 30
Gaviola, Bishop M., 36
Ghana, 19, 25; missionaries to, 14, 26, 31, 40
Goa (India), 46
God's Witness in the Heart of the World (Boff), 78
Gregory XVI, 2
Grenada, 26
Guatemala, 40
Haiti, 59; missionaries to, 30, 40
Handmaids of the Child Jesus, 30
Hanoi, 54
Himo (Tanzania), 33
Hinduism, 34, 43, 56
Hindus, 47
Holy Spirit Fathers, 18, 29, 30
Hong Kong, 37; missionaries to, 40, 62
I.C.M. Sisters, 14, 19, 20, 40, 48, 49
Iglesias sin Fronteras, 65
Immaculate Heart of Mary Mission Society. *See* C.I.C.M. Fathers
Imperialism, 69
Inculturation: of Asian missionaries, 35; of Indian missionaries, 45; of international missionary organziations, 86, 88; and the option for the poor, 77; of Western and third church missionaries, 74-81
India, 13, 14, 18, 55, 88; Catholic population of, 43; Christian population of, 43; Eastern-rite Catholics in, 44-45; indigenous congregations and institutes in, 19, 43-44; methods of training seminarians in, 78-79; missionaries from, 8, 14, 20, 40, 46, 49, 85; missionaries to, 20, 40, 56; number of bishops in, 43; number of brothers in, 43; number of lay workers in, 44; number of priests in, 43, 45; number of secular institutes in, 44; number of seminarians in, 44; number of sisters in, 17, 37, 43, 44; population of, 34, 42; theological reviews in, 47; *see also* Kerala, state of (India)
Indian Missiological Review, 47
Indian Missionary Society, 46
Indian Theological Studies, 47
Indigenization: in Asia, 34; in India, 88; of international missionary institutes, 19, 74
Individualism, Western, 83
Indonesia, 14, 37; missionaries to, 40, 62
Institute of Our Lady of Guadalupe for Foreign Missions, 62
International Congress on Mission (Manila), 40-42
Iperu (Nigeria), 28
Ireland, 17
Ishvan Kendra (India), 47
Islam, 23, 34, 43, 56, 72
Italy, 15, 16, 31, 44; missionaries to, 26, 31
Ivory Coast, 25, 26
Japan, 37, 52, 73, 85; missionaries from, 52-53; missionaries to, 40, 62
Jeevadhara, 47
Jesuits: and African countries, 29, 49, 63; and Asian countries, 13, 18, 20, 40, 47, 49, 53; and the Fiji Islands, 49; and Latin American countries, 49, 63; methods of training, in India, 79; as working in international teams, 84
Jesus Christ, 65, 66, 74, 84, 89; and Asia, 36; and Latin America, 58, 69; and the poor, 80; and Western missionaries, 1
John Paul II: and Africa, 25-27; on Brazilian mission, 64-65; on *Evangelii Nuntiandi*, 8; on missionary vocations, 11; on Philippine mission, 38-39; on priestly vocations, 59; third church affecting election of, 12
John XXIII, 57
Kalilombe, Bishop P., 8
Kamed (India), 47
Kampala, 10, 24, 25
Kenosis, 74, 87
Kenya: missionaries to, 26, 28, 31, 49, 62; novices in, 18, 32, 33; novitiates in, 32; seminarians in, 32; sisters in, 28, 30, 31; training houses in, 33; vocations in, 27; *see also* AMECEA
Kerala, state of (India), 44-45, 46
Kim Nal Su, Bishop, 51
Kinshasa, 24, 25
Kiserian (Kenya), 32
Korea, 37, 50, 51; missionaries from, 51; missionaries to, 40, 56, 62

Index

Korean Missionary Society, 51
Kottar (India), 46
Kottayam (India), 44
Kumasi (Ghana), 25
Kyoto, 37
Lagos (Nigeria), 26
Langata (Kenya), 32
Latin America, 82; *ad extra* evangelization in, 59, 61, 69; *ad intra* evangelization in, 61; basic ecclesial communities in, 59, 61, 67, 68; Catholic population of, 12, 57; missionaries from, 85; missionaries to, 20, 40, 46, 52, 56, 85; missionary training centers in, 61; national mission congresses in, 60; number of bishops in, 12; number of dioceses in, 12; number of priestly ordinations in, 15; number of priests in, 15, 60; number of seminarians in, 16, 58-59; number of sisters in, 17; option for the poor in, 57-58; population of, 16, 42; ratio of population to priests in, 16-17
Latin American Conference of Religious. *See* CLAR
Latin American Episcopal Conference. *See* CELAM
Lay missionaries, 40, 76
Lazarists, 29
Liberation theology, 58, 80
Liberia, 26
Lima, 61, 67
Little Brothers of Charles de Foucauld, 54
Little Flower Congregation, 45
Little Flower Mission League, 45
Local church as sending church: in Brazil, 63; and international missionary institutes, 82; in Latin America, 67, 68; in the Philippines, 41-42; responsibility of, 90; Vatican II on, 3-4, 81, 89; *see also* Fidei Donum priests
Localization, 30, 74-75
Luanda, Archbishop of, 62
Lumen Gentium, 3, 5, 21, 91
Madagascar, 29; missionaries to, 30
Mahagi diocese (Zaire), 62
Malagasay, 29
Malawi, 31
Malaysia, 20, 56
Manaus (Brazil), 64
Manila, 10, 37, 38, 40
Manila Conference (International Congress on Mission), 40-42
Marengoni, Father G., 32
Mark, Saint, 9
Maryknoll, 11, 19, 40, 62
Mauritius, 30, 49
Maximum Illud, 2
Mazzoldi, Bishop S., 32
Medellín, Archbishop of, 63

Medellín Conference (Second General Conference of Latin American Bishops), 9, 58, 59, 66
M.E.P. Fathers. *See* Foreign Missions of Paris
Mexico, 60, 61-62; missionaries from, 62, 65-66; missionaries to, 40
Missiology, 6, 47
Missionaries of the Consolata, 19
Missionary Brothers of Charity, 48-49, 87
Missionary Sisters of Charity, 48-49, 87
Missionary Sisters of Jesus Crucified, 64
Missionary Sisters of St. Charles Borromeo, 14
Missionary Sisters of St. Theresa, 62
Missionary Sisters of the Immaculate Heart of Mary, 13, 49
Missionary Society of St. Paul, 28
Missionary Society of St. Thomas the Apostle, 45, 47
Missionary Society of the Philippines, 39
Mission Sunday, 64
Moroto (Uganda), 28
Mother Teresa, 48-49
Mozambique, 64
Munive Escobar, Bishop L., 61
Muslims, 47
Mutuae Relationes, 91
Nadiket (Uganda), 32
Nairobi, 32
National, Biblical, Catechetical, and Liturgical Center of Bangalore, 47
National Commission for Evangelization (Vietnam), 54
Nationalism of missionaries, 84
Near East, 52
Neminem Profecto, 2
Neocolonialism, 73
Nepal, 49, 53
New Guinea, 40, 51
New Zealand, 13
Nguyen, Archbishop Kim Dien, 54
Nigeria, 18, 27, 28, 29, 31; missionaries from, 26, 30, 31; missionaries to, 30, 40, 42
Norbertines, 29
"Norms for the Cooperation of Local Churches among Themselves and Especially for a Better Distribution of the Clergy in the World," 16
North America, 57; Catholic population of, 12; missionaries from, 1, 85; missionaries to, 48, 85; number of dioceses in, 12; number of priestly ordinations in, 15; number of priests in, 15; number of seminarians in, 16; number of sisters in, 17; population of, 42; ratio of population to priests in, 16
Nyerere, Julius, 77

Index

Oblate Fathers, 20, 29, 40
Oceania, 82; missionaries from, 85; missionaries to, 85; number of bishops in, 12; number of priestly ordinations in, 15; number of priests in, 15; number of seminarians in, 16; number of sisters in, 17
Ongata Rongai training house (Kenya), 33
Option for the poor, 82; and the Asian church, 35, 37; and the Latin American church, 57-58, 69; theology and, 80; and third church missionaries, 76-81
Ortunga, Cardinal, 32
Our Lady of Guadalupe, 61
Pakistan, 20, 49, 56
Palai diocese (India), 44
Pallu, Bishop François, 1
Pan-African Episcopal Council, 64
Paraguay, 40
Particular churches, doctrine of, 3-6
Patronato (Padroado) system, 1
Paul, Saint, 5
Paul VI: on African mission, 10, 24-25; on Asian mission, 10, 36-37; and FABC, 35; on missions to Africa, 25; and Nigerian mission, 28; on Philippine missionary vocations, 11; on third church mission, 8
People's Republic of the Congo, 26, 30
Perfectae Caritatis, 21, 91
Peru, 59, 60
Peruvian Association for Missionaries, 65
Philippine Lay Mission Volunteers, 40
Philippines, the, 13, 14, 39-40, 55, 85; Catholic population of, 34, 38; missionaries from, 20, 39-40, 42; missionaries to, 62; number of bishops in, 38; number of cardinals in, 38; number of priests in, 38; number of seminarians in, 38; number of sisters in, 37, 38; Paul VI's visit to, 36; ratio of population to priests in, 16-17
Picachy, Cardinal, 8
Pieris, Aloysius, 80
Pinto, Father Gaspar, 46
Pius XI, 2, 11, 38, 84
Pius XII, 11, 21, 91
Poland, 15, 16, 17, 44, 54, 55, 70
Ponmundi (India), 36
Pontifical Mission Aid Societies, 18, 41; and Brazilian mission, 63, 64; in Colombia, 63; and Latin America, 60-61, 69; publishing *Revista de Misiones*, 62; role of, 70; third church influence in, 13; and Vietnam, 54
Poor Clares of the Blessed Sacrament, 62
Portugal, 1, 2, 75
Poverty. *See* Option for the poor
Priests, number of in the world, 15
Princeps Pastorum, 11
Priory of the Resurrection (Zaire), 18
Propaganda Fide (1622), 1
Puebla Conference (Third General Conference of Latin American Bishops), 58, 60, 66-67
Radio Veritas, 39
Ranchi district (India), 13
Rejaf (Sudan), 32
Relationes in Territoriis Missionum, 91
Religious men, number of in the world, 17
Religious priests, proportion of diocesan priests to, 17
Religious women, number of in the world, 17
Rerum Ecclesiae, 2, 11
Reúnion, 30
Revista de Misiones, 62
Rio de Janeiro, 59, 64
Rome, 10, 82
Rosales, Bishop G., 41, 42
Ruhuna, bishop, 27
Rwanda, 24, 29, 32; missionaries to, 27
Sacred Congregation for Bishops, 91
Sacred Congregation for Religious and Secular Institutes, 77, 91
Sacred Congregation for the Clergy, 16
Sacred Congregation for the Evangelization of Peoples, 17, 84, 91
Saigon, 53
St. Peter Pontifical Seminary (Bangalore), 47
Salesian Fathers, 18, 29, 40, 47, 49
Sangu, Bishop J., 79
SECAM, 10, 80
Second Vatican Council. *See* Vatican II
Seoul, 36
Servants of the Immaculate Heart of Mary. *See* Sisters of the Good Shepherd
Sierra Leone, 31; missionaries to, 26, 31, 62
Sikhism, 43
Sisters, number of in the world, 17
Sisters of Mother Teresa. *See* Missionary Sisters of Charity
Sisters of Notre Dame, 53
Sisters of Our Lady of Kilimanjaro, 18, 28, 30
Sisters of St. Anne, 48
Sisters of St. Paul de Chartres, 40
Sisters of the Good Shepherd, 40
Sisters of the Immaculate Heart of Mary 18, 31, 52, 53
Sisters of Verona, 33
Society of Pilar, 46
Society of the Divine Word. *See* S.V.D. Fathers
Society of the Missionaries of St. Francis Xavier, 46
South Africa, 30

Spain, 1, 2, 75
Sri Lanka, 13, 47, 55-56, 85; missionaries from, 20, 56
Sudan, 32, 49. *See also* AMECEA
S.V.D. Fathers, 13, 19, 40, 47
Symposium of Episcopal Conferences of Africa and Madagascar, 10, 80
Synod of bishops (1974), 6-11, 24, 36, 52, 81, 91
Synod of bishops (1977), 7
Synod of bishops (1980), 7
Syro-Malabars (Eastern-rite Catholics), 44-45, 47
Syro-Malankars (Eastern-rite Catholics), 44
Tagaytay (Philippines), 40
Taipei Conference (FABC), 10, 35, 36, 46
Taiwan, 30, 40
Tamil Nadu (India), 46
Tanzania, 18, 19, 28, 30, 32, 33; Moshi diocese (Tanzania); increase of vocations in, 27; missionaries from, 28, 30; missionaries to, 27, 49; *see also* AMECEA
Theology, 12-13, 79-80. *See also* Liberation theology
Third church, definition of, ix, xn.1
Third World: members of Roman Curia from, 12; number of bishops from, 12; number of cardinals from, 12; number of dioceses in, 12; number of priestly ordinations in, 15; number of priests in, 15; number of seminarians in, 16; number of sisters in, 17
Third World church, definition of, xn.1
Tlaxcala (Mexico), 60
Tokyo, 36
Torreón (Mexico), 60
Tran Dinh Thy, Father Dominique Marie, 54
Uganda, 18, 19, 32, 33; increase of vocations in, 27; missionaries to, 27; *see also* AMECEA
Ujjan diocese (India), 45
United States, the, 44, 54; missionaries to, 30, 40
Ursulines of Tildonck, 48
Uru (Tanzania), 32

Uruguay, 66
Vatican II: and *ad extra* mission, 62; and African missionary consciousness, 24; Asian and African bishops at, 2; on bishops and religious institutes, 90-91; on bishops' responsibility for mission, 90; on exchange of diocesan priests, 21; on inculturation of missionaries, 74; and indigenization of the church, 6; and intercultural dialogue, 73; and Latin American church, 57, 58, 68; on local churches and mission, 81, 89; and Medellín Conference, 9; on mission, 41; on religious institutes and local churches, 22; and Sri Lanka church, 56; and third church mission, 2-6, 11
Venezuela, 46, 59
Vidyajyoti, 47
Vietcong, the, 54
Vietnam, 53-55, 85, 87; missionaries from, 14; number of seminarians in, 16; number of sisters from, 37
Vietnamese Missionary Society, 54
Vincentian Congregation, 45
Walsh, Father James A., 11
Western world: number of priestly ordinations in, 15; number of seminarians in, 16
White Fathers, 19, 29, 84
White Sisters, 19
World, population of the, 72
World Mission Sunday, 37
Xaverian Missionaries of Yarumal, 62
Xaverian Missionary Fathers, 19
Xavier Mission House, 46
Zaire, 14, 18, 19; Catholic population of, 24; increase of vocations in, 27; John Paul II's visit to, 25; missionaries from, 11, 30; missionaries to, 27, 30, 40, 49, 62; number of clerical religious institutes in, 29; number of congregations of sisters in, 18; number of novices in, 29; number of priests in, 30; number of seminarians in, 29
Zambia: missionaries to, 26, 30, 40; *See also* AMECEA